A Girl's Pocket Guide to Trouser Trout

Reflections on Dating and Fly-Fishing

By

Gail Rubin

ISBN: 1-4140-1280-2 (e-book)
ISBN: 1-4140-1279-9 (Paperback)

Library of Congress Control Number: 2003097316

This book is printed on acid free paper.

Printed in the United States of America
Bloomington, IN

1stBooks – rev. 02/02/04

To Dave, my trophy trout.
You prove that trouser trout angling works.

Acknowledgements

My thanks to the many people who helped make this book a reality.

To Jim and Elizabeth "Boo" Cochran for your friendship and a fortuitous pit stop trip into the woods that sparked it all.

To the members of the Intrepid critique group – Patty Allred, Sherri Burr, Ella Joan Fenoglio, Kathleen Hessler, Kay Lamb, Sue Mann, Jeane McKenna, Donna Pedace, Susan Wyatt, and others before them. Your input helped enormously.

To the SouthWest Writers organization and the hard working people who keep it running, for programs that inspire and inform writers of all kinds.

To all of the wonderful trouser trout and unbelievable Other Fish in the Sea I have dated, thanks for giving me so much material to work with.

And to Mom—thanks for the advice.

TABLE OF CONTENTS

Introduction

Trouser Trout Fishing in America: An Overview

Starting to fly fish for trout is like falling in love. The early gratifications, be they kisses or rising trout, are heady and decidedly unscientific. They exist of the moment, and for the moment, that's enough. Sooner or later things calm down a little, and as the infatuation continues you want to know more.

John Merwin, *The New American Trout Fishing*

When I was a teenager crying over a breakup with my first boyfriend, my mother told me there were plenty of fish in the sea. Little did I know what she was really referring to... trouser trout are everywhere.

What's a trouser trout? He's the excellent catch a woman wants to land. He's that shining being who makes your heart jump when you first connect. He's a keeper. A trouser trout is a good man, with the other-worldly appeal of the opposite sex.

A Girl's Pocket Guide to Trouser Trout is your how-to guide to landing a lunker. A lunker in angling parlance is a very fine fish. If you're not familiar with the lingo of the fishing world, or don't recognize how a term applies to trouser trout angling, you can look it up in the glossary in the back of this book.

The idea for *A Girl's Pocket Guide to Trouser Trout* was spawned high in the mountains of southern Colorado in a cabin with a group of friends. After a feast featuring plenty of merlot and after-dinner liqueurs, we brainstormed the topic of trouser trout and fishing for men. I laughed so hard my face hurt. And I took four pages of notes.

The next day, when sober, most of the material was still rather funny. But it wasn't until I started reading up on trout fishing that the truth hit home. There's a remarkable connection between men and fish, and the tango of angler and trout strongly resembles human relationships.

Fly-fishing elicits participant passion unrivaled in most other sports. Over five thousand books have been published in the English language alone on fly-fishing, probably the most extensive literature on any one sport. In the last decade of the 20th century, hundreds of books were published about fly-fishing and on dating and relationships. This is not a coincidence.

While reading various books on trout fishing, I was struck by the descriptions of fish such as the athletic rainbow, the wily brown, the migratory sea trout and the amiable lake trout.

"Wait a minute," I thought, "I've dated guys like these." Whether the quarry is a man or a fish, angling requires patience, persistence, practice, a good dose of finesse, subtlety, knowledge, and a sense of humor.

With thousands of women now joining the ranks of active anglers, let's recognize that women and fishing go together in more ways than one. Women are trouser trout anglers, hitting the streams to land a lunker. Yet, there were no how-to books on trouser trout angling, until now.

As the world's foremost expert on trouser trout angling, I cast this collection of advice upon the waters, in the hopes that others may benefit from these bits of wisdom. My fly-fishing knowledge is primarily from reading, but my trouser trout knowledge comes from hard-won personal experience.

When people ask how long I've been fishing, I say I've been trouser trout angling for over 25 years. I met my first husband when I was 18, got married at 23, divorced at 28, then landed my trophy trout and got married to my second husband at 42.

I have swum many laps in the treacherous waters of the dating pool. After so many relationships, I got the lifetime achievement award for catch and release fishing. I've braved long dry spells between relation-ships, and juggled dating several men at one time. After years of casting for a good catch and mourning several that got away, I finally landed a keeper.

Fly-fishing provides ample relationship metaphors that apply to both men and fish. Many innocent passages in fly-fishing books and angling journals contain solid information for dating and relationships. Throughout this book, quotes from the greats and the unknowns of the angling world provide good advice on our favorite quarry, the trouser trout.

* * *

And therefore, to all you that are virtuous, gentle and freeborn, I write and make this simple treatise which follows, by which you can have the whole art of angling to amuse you as you please, in order that your age may flourish the more and last the longer.

Dame Juliana Berners,
The Treatise of Fishing with an Angle

Over five hundred years ago, Dame Juliana Berners, a nun and noblewoman, wrote the first instructional fishing text in the English language: *The Treatise of Fishing with an Angle*. It's estimated Dame Juliana first wrote down her angling observations in Hertfordshire, England about 1421-25, more than two hundred years before Izaak Walton wrote his fly-fishing classic *The Compleat Angler* in 1653.

One of history's all-time best sellers, *The Compleat Angler* presents a mellow philosophy of life along with trout fishing tips. Reprinted at least three hundred times, at one point its sales were only exceeded by the Bible and *Pilgrims Progress*. From the fifteenth century to today's monthly magazines, trout fishing continues to be a thoroughly dissected topic.

Dame Juliana's treatise was printed about 1496 as part of the second edition of *The Book of St. Albans*, a nobleman's primer on hunting, fishing and heraldry. *The Book of St. Albans* is memorable for its colorful terms for groups of animals: an exaltation of larks, a bouquet of pheasants, a knot of toads, and a murder of crows. And when you catch several fish, it's called a brace of trout. You should be so lucky.

Dame Juliana's treatise goes into mind-numbing, eye-glazing detail (to a non-angler) on creating imitation flies that fish will bite, using materials such as fur, feathers, wool, and silk. She also specifies when, where and how to use them and recommends the proper attitude for approaching angling. Dame Juliana calls angling a pleasure and a recreation to be treasured and conserved by well-meaning individuals.

Doesn't that sound like today's trouser trout angling? Don't we anglers dress up in silk, wool or leather to lure some trout's attention? Aren't we stalking the streams in which an available lunker might lurk? Don't we cast about to land a good catch? Isn't it true that girls just want to have fun?

A confirmation of the connection between man and trout comes to us from the highlands of Scotland, where there are manly men and much great fishing for brown trout and salmon. At Scottish weddings in some communities, the groom will wear an artificial fly instead of a flower as a boutonniere, to indicate he'd been "hooked." They may wear kilts, but that just gives their favorite fish room to move (and gives the local anglers easy access).

As we travel this wide wet world of trouser trout angling, we'll touch on desirable types of trout, Other Fish in the Sea to avoid, where the lunkers lurk, how to get their attention and land your catch. We'll visit with trouser trout anglers who have some big fish stories to tell, examine issues about angling as we get older and explore some of the reasons the fish stop biting.

When dating, women are no longer the passive fly or the underwater nymph waiting for the trout to cruise by and take the bait. *A Girl's Pocket Guide to Trouser Trout* will show you how to master the art of trouser trout angling so you can choose your lure, make your cast, and reel those rascals in!

You get a line, I'll get a pole, honey
You get a line, I'll get a pole, darlin'
You get a line, I'll get a pole
We'll go down to the fishin' hole
Un-huh, un-huh, uh-huh!
             The Crawdad Song

It will be a true pleasure to see the fair, bright, shining-scaled fishes outwitted by your crafty means and drawn out on the land.

             Dame Juliana Berners,
      The Treatise of Fishing with an Angle

Chapter One

Your Personal Angling Style

Amy, Margo and Helen, all 30-something, educated, attractive single women, bask in the sun on the beach, watching the parade of trouser trout go by.

Margo, a red-headed, fair-skinned divorcee, constantly trolls for available trout.

Helen, an incurable flirt, uses her blonde hair to draw attention away from her generous thighs.

Amy, petite, brunette, and fresh from a break up, despairs about ever reeling in someone suitable, let alone bagging a trophy trout.

"Ooh, he's cute," cooed Margo as she ogled a well-sculpted fellow splashing through the surf.

"Look at that gold chain, c'mon," said Amy. "And he's way too hairy."

"Hairy is good. Shows he's got testosterone. No Viagra needed…usually," quipped Helen.

"Is sex all you want?" said Amy.

"No, I want looks, money, smarts, kindness, caring, communication, a sense of humor… and sex," said Helen.

"I want a man to be the friend I can tell everything to," said Amy.

"You have us to tell everything to," said Margo.

"I don't want to have sex with you," said Amy.

Amy surveyed the beach, watching three guys play Frisbee nearby, leaping and diving after the plastic toy.

"Why do we do this at all," she mused.

The Frisbee sails in their direction. Helen, still lounging on the sand, reaches one hand up and snatches it. "Can we play too?" she inquired of the nearest young man.

The epitome of troutly manhood, he cheerfully replied, "Well, sure. Why not?"

The innocent game of Frisbee led to an afternoon of social frivolity and an evening of beachside dining and dancing, proffering the promise of blossoming summer romance.

* * *

Afterward, the lucky fisherwomen said a grateful prayer to the Trout Goddess for the fortuitous catch while their boatboys pumped up their chests pridefully and mentally took all the credit.

Sally I. Stoner, *Women in the Stream*

Why We Go Fishing

Why do trouser trout anglers pursue trout? Why couldn't these women just relax and enjoy a day at the beach without focusing their energy on the opposite sex? Why go fishing at all?

Gloria Steinem's feminist slogan "A woman without a man is like a fish without a bicycle" rings ever more true with each advance women make in our society. But a woman with a buff lunker in bicycle pants probably smiles a lot more.

Fly fishers are an avid bunch, and trouser trout anglers are just as passionate about their sport. A major sporting magazine survey indicated that most men said they go fishing just to get out of the house. What motivates millions of women to go out trouser trout angling? Let's examine some reasons to go fishing, as applied to the hunt for trouser trout.

Food

One of the prime activities in dating, the ancient dance of trouser trout and angler, is eating out. Everyone's got to eat – why not eat together? As every good Jewish mother knows, food is sharing and caring. Food is a concrete expression of love served up on a daily basis.

Many of us hate eating alone, especially a fine meal. Dining alone, we read a book, magazine, newspaper, mail, or watch TV, anything to avoid staring blankly at the walls, like Dave the suddenly-ancient astronaut at the end of *2001: A Space Odyssey*. How depressing that was.

Dining out together gives the angler fine insights into a fellow's manners, his eloquence, cuisine preferences, even the way he makes choices. Lunch is a safe first-time outing, shorter and cheaper than a dinner date. A daytime rendezvous that does not go well can be cut short by afternoon activities. The angler can avoid the open-ended nature of evening hours after a dismal dinner experience.

As society has evolved to allow women elevated earning power, interesting dilemmas and struggles have ensued over who pays and under what circumstances. Call me old-fashioned, but he should pay for the first three dates if he asks you out. It shows he's serious about seeing you.

If you ask him out, you can pick up the check or have a friendly disagreement about who pays. If he asks you out and you wind up paying or you split the bill, he's cheap, broke or ambivalent about you. In a well-established relationship, you can pick up the check without threatening his manhood.

If an angler has dinner out and happily winds up with breakfast in bed the next morning, she's had a very successful fishing trip.

Gail Rubin

Companionship

There are two types of companionship modes for trouser trout trolling: girls' night out and the search for a trophy trout of one's own.

Girls' night out appeals primarily to younger anglers. Nightlife in a group with other trouser trout anglers can be an amusing way to spend an evening, even if your clothes do stink of cigarette smoke when you get home. Bars are popular fishing streams, places where all sorts of social circles intersect.

The camaraderie of being out with your Wild Wahini friends, dancing, flirting, drinking and talking, all make for fun memories when you're in the Old Angler Home.

It's the second mode, the drive for lifelong companionship with one trophy trout that compels so many anglers to hit the streams. We go fishing to fill the urge to share our life with another. We fish to find the one with whom we can laugh and talk, share joys, sorrows, adventures and the everyday rhythm of living, to eat, sleep, love and live together.

Pacific salmon, a relative of the trout, mate for life in that they die after spawning. Humans are blessed, or cursed, depending on your point of view, to see many mornings-after once the urges of a lust-crazed night have been fulfilled. You can wake up with someone you really care about or someone who just seemed like a good idea at the time, and that time has passed.

In most fishing competitions, bigger is better. However, when considering the trophy trouser trout, personality counts. The qualities that make a man a trophy trout are unique to each angler.

One angler's trout to be taken home and mounted for posterity might be a dead fish to you or me. Important details like values, interests, humor, intelligence, compatibility, and personal habits make the difference between a keeper and one that gets tossed back.

While we troll for the finest-looking trouser trout we can find, it's the ones that make us laugh, share our values and provide good company that usually win our hearts, whether they're lunkers or fingerlings, handsome or homely. The anglers who find the keepers for life are lucky. The rest of us continue returning to the streams, hoping to hook that shining being who will be our heart's delight.

Sport

Some gals, just like guys, engage in dating just for the thrill of the hunt. They practice catch and release fishing exclusively. They like flirting, getting the interest of some fine-looking lunker, playing with them for a while and then letting them go. Anglers on a girls' night out often participate in sport fishing.

The sport angler may be an intellectual who tires when the conversation gets stale. She may be a sexual gymnast who regularly needs a fresh pommel horse. Perhaps she wants different guys for different reasons: his mind, his money, his humor, or his trout. Maybe he lives in another town and neither wants to move.

She may be insecure and tosses back many good catches because she doesn't feel he's good enough, or perhaps that she's not good enough. A sporty angler can inflict a lot of pain on the unsuspecting trouser trout that gets his heart hooked.

What if this angler's catch will not allow himself to be casually tossed back? Suppose he decides, once landed, that he's into the start of something long-term?
Singer/songwriter Chris LeDoux summed it up nicely when he sang, "What'cha gonna do with a cowboy when he don't saddle up and ride away?"

The sporting angler can get caught in her own lines if she's not careful. If he decides to hang around, she'll need a metaphorical crowbar to pry him off and get him moving along.

Spawning

Men, women and fish all heed the call of the wild at some point, striking with abandon when the spawning urge hits. While spawning is not really a reason to go fishing, it is a strong motivator for trouser trout angling.

Fish have their specific season to spawn, but humans are ready to rock just about anytime. Spawning trout, in their struggle to reach their native waters for a little reproductive satisfaction, lose weight, their eyes bulge out and their teeth protrude. Thank goodness we don't do that. Well, most of us don't. Well, we are constantly concerned about our weight. Hmm…

Humans can spawn for procreation, but more often spawning is for fun. It feels good and we get very cranky if we don't do it.

Many (not all) women, and even some men, crave having children and get frantic if they haven't procreated before the biological clock winds down. I've not observed a visceral paternal urge in men, but noted most will leap at the chance to indulge in the feel-good motive.

Thanks to reliable birth control and the sexual revolution, women can also enjoy sex simply because it feels good, if that's what they want (see Sport).

In this dangerous age of scary sexually transmitted diseases, reckless spawning now delivers major anxiety and potentially devastating consequences. The smart active angler uses condoms (more on this later).

Some anglers retreat into celibacy to avoid the issue. Don't be fooled by their pious protestations. Like seeds in the desert waiting to sprout after a good soaking rain, the spawning urge is still lurking in the background, ready to leap front and center given the slightest stimulation.

Money

Cash-award fishing tournaments are rare in fly-fishing circles. Yet, in the hunt for trouser trout, the money motive almost always lurks there in the reptilian part of women's brains. It's left over from cave-dwelling times. Is he a good provider? Is he going to drag home the meat? This thought lingers in the female brain, even if we're bringing home the bacon on our own, thank you very much.

The image of gold diggers may be tarnished, but the pursuit of the golden trout, also known as a sugar daddy, is still vigorous. The dream of finding someone handsome, smart, funny, considerate, and rich, is all too often an impossible dream.

A fellow's politics may be insulting, his manners and taste appalling, his conversation one-sided, but his money is oh-so-green and the things it can buy make a relationship palatable. As Cyndi Lauper aptly put it, "Money changes everything."

Back in the 1400s, our fishing expert Dame Juliana cautioned anglers on their ethics, saying "You must not use this aforesaid artful sport for covetousness, merely for the increasing or saving of your money, but for your enjoyment and to procure the health of your body, and more especially, of your soul."

Even 500 years ago, she cautioned against greed and encouraged the positive physical, mental, and spiritual aspects of angling. A man can be a trophy trout without a fat wallet.

Gail Rubin

Inspirational Scenery

One of the best things about angling is getting outdoors into some truly spectacular sites in nature. The sound of moving water, the glint of sunlight, the soothing balm of green trees and grass is all part of trout fishing's lyric lure. While one can go trouser trout trolling in such bucolic settings, if you're after an angler who's after a fish, he's not going to pay much attention to you, at least not until he's finished fishing for the day.

Most trouser trout trolling is done in settings where the environmental scenery is perhaps not quite as attractive, but the human scenery is paramount. Isn't people-watching a blast? It isn't just the way guys look but how they act and what they say that makes them such fascinating creatures.

Someone with washboard abs, killer biceps and pecs to die for may be fun to look at, but if he's a jerk or totally blank between the ears, do you really want to spend much time with him? Okay, maybe on a catch and release basis. It never hurts to look, but, as my mother said, looks aren't everything.

Even with all these reasons to go fishing, some insecure anglers approach trouser trout trolling with the attitude that they don't deserve to catch a trophy trout. Hogwash. You don't find fishermen questioning whether they deserve to catch a fish. It's an angler's God-given right, perfectly natural and legal, providing you have a license. If the fish takes the lure and gets hooked, it's the angler's lucky day.

And the trouser trout benefits too. Studies show that married men live longer than unmarried guys.

Ladies, carefully study and cultivate this attitude. You have a right to a happy, fulfilling relationship. Whatever your looks, upbringing, intelligence, in any area of your life, cast your line without reservation into endeavors you wish to undertake. When you look back on your life, you'll regret the things you didn't do more than the ones you did. You certainly won't catch anything if you don't get your line out on the water.

Types of Anglers

Among the growing numbers of those who call themselves fly-fishers, I have rarely met the man of casual approach. No, the hunt for trout is a force which pulses in the blood, fills the mind with nostalgic recollection and new hopes.

Joe Brooks, *Trout Fishing*

Women have different angling styles, reflecting the varied reasons to hit the streams for trouser trout. Angling motivations and tactics are unique to each woman. Anglers can be honest straight-shooters and game-playing manipulators, quiet homebodies and good-time party girls, independent career women and full-time mothers. The dance of angler and trout is an endlessly variable tango, thanks to the wide differences in female psyches and trouser trout qualities.

Here are a few of the most popular angling styles, based on archetypal psychological profiles created by Jungian psychologist Jean Shinoda Bolen. In her landmark book, *Goddesses in Everywoman*, she identified seven major psychological profiles associated with the attributes of major Greek goddesses.

See if you don't recognize yourself or someone you know in these descriptions.

The Love Queen (Aphrodite) is an imaginative, unpredictable, creative and compelling angler. Even if she's plain looking, she has a magnetic warmth and sensuality that draws men into her life. She exudes a golden glow that makes people feel special, but her attention span may be short. She's a great entertainer, livening up any social event with dancing, singing and storytelling, but her fun-loving nature may be distracting and non-productive in a work setting.

She is likely to snag a trout for spawning because it feels good and she enjoys the relationship, not necessarily because she wants to have children, although babies may result from her active love life. She's also more likely to be a sport fisher, a catch and release angler who turns a trout loose when he no longer amuses her.

The Great Outdoors Woman (Artemis) is an independent angler who sets her sights on what she wants and shoots for her goals. This achievement-oriented gal enjoys the great outdoors, hiking, camping and generally communing with nature. She is especially happy when next to or swimming in any lovely body of water.

She can be happy in the company of women friends, but will also seek male companionship, someone with whom she can share enjoyment of the scenery. She's another sport fisher, with tendencies toward catch and release relationships. When she does hook up with a man, she will seek a trout who's her equal or who provides a balance to her abilities and interests.

The Intellectual Angler (Athena) indulges in civilized, thoughtful pursuits like concerts, theater, museums and the other cultural attractions big city life offers. Often emotionally distant while intellectually active, if she decides she wants a trophy trout, she'll survey the situation and develop a strategy to land her catch.

Her angling incentive is companionship with a powerful, perceptive, intelligent man, but she may also be drawn by money. She is often attracted to heroes, successful men, and leaders in business or politics.

The Great Mother (Demeter) is an angler who embodies the nurturing Mom in every woman. She wants to take care of others, physically, emotionally, or spiritually. She's absolutely devoted to children and may focus her loving attention on pets if she doesn't have children.

She's supportive and helpful, sometimes overly so, bossing others with her opinions of the right way to do things. She may give others so much she risks losing herself in the process. Her motives for angling are spawning for children, or perhaps to land a man she can mother and smother with food.

The Stand-By-Your-Man Angler (Hera) wants to be married and won't feel complete until she lands her trophy trout. More than companionship, her motive is completion. This angler sees her husband as the fulfillment of her life, and once she makes a commitment, woe to anyone who interferes with the union.

If her husband turns out to be a philanderer, the fault always lies with the other woman, never with him. While she finds great fulfillment as a married woman, she is devastated when death or divorce breaks the union apart.

The Great Home Spirit Angler (Hestia) is a quiet, calm woman, an introvert with a spiritual glow. Her home is a cheerful sanctuary where she finds peace in solitude and orderliness. She radiates compassion, wisdom, centering, and warmth.

This self-sufficient woman can be very happy on her own. If she does land a trout for companionship or spawning reasons, he's likely to be an extrovert, balancing her introversion.

The Innocent Maiden Angler (Persephone) is a compliant, dependent type of woman who seems to wait for someone or something to transform her life. She's a "good girl," a quiet child-woman who may be abnormally close to her mother. Her quiet exterior hides a deep connection to other worlds of dreams and visions.

She may not seek to land a trout, but her passivity can be an attractor. The kinds of men who are drawn to her include inexperienced fingerlings, tough guys who want to protect her and men uncomfortable with assertive adult women. She can also be a target for Other Fish in the Sea, particularly urchins, octopus, shellfish and blowfish (more about Other Fish in Chapter Two).

Most women's personal angling styles incorporate a combination of these archetypal motivations, which ebb and flow over time. Some motivations, such as a longing to have children or a desire for solitude, will assert themselves strongly at specific times in a woman's life.

Something as basic as the monthly menstrual cycle can throw a woman's demeanor for a loop. PMS can turn even the most mild-mannered woman into a cranky, weepy, chocolate-obsessed gorgon (one of three snaky-haired sisters of Greek mythology whose glance turns the beholder to stone).

Demeanor dictates how trouser trout anglers approach the quarry, select and deploy their lures, and cast their lines. But before we get into those details, let's look at the object of our affection: the trout himself.

Chapter Two

Types of Trout and Other Fish in the Sea

Frank is an eligible, modern kind of guy. A busy CPA and a connoisseur of fine wine, cooking and photography, he keeps in shape swimming laps at the Y three times a week. He always arrives at 6:00 a.m. before the retired ladies show up for water aerobics.

An attractive brunette woman swims almost every day he's there. He watches her each time they pass, taking in her strong legs, swimmer's shoulders and trim physique. She's a good swimmer, keeping up with his brisk pace. One day, they finish about the same time, and emerge dripping from the pool.

While drying off, she says, "You do the back stroke well. I like to vary it with the breast stroke, but it takes longer to do."

Frank's eyes are magnetically drawn to her perky nipples calling out from her clingy tank suit. A bulge starts building in his Speedo suit. He quickly wraps a towel around his waist and says, "Would you like to continue our conversation with clothes on sometime?"

They agree to meet in the lobby and exchange phone numbers. Amy smiles. His swimsuit revealed she has a cutthroat on the line.

* * *

Types of Trout

The trout, however, is not so much difficult as misunderstood.

John Merwin, *The New American Trout Fishing*

There are over two-dozen types of trout fish in the world, including salmonoid relatives of salmon, char, and whitefish. Fishermen sing the praises of chasing rainbow, brown, cutthroat and other fishy family members. The types of trouser trout are equally varied. We shall sing songs of the trouser trout, in their glorious range of variety, comparing them to salmonoids by personality and physical attributes.

Consider: both are highly sought quarry, some notoriously difficult to catch. Slim-built, well-muscled and hard-fighting describes both men and fish in their prime. Both do things to baffle and infuriate anglers, and are frequently the object of obsessive behavior.

Like humans, trout have been transplanted from their native waters to flourish in other parts of the world. And both have been celebrated in words and art through the centuries.

However, a fish won't warm your feet when you put your freezing tootsies on his back during a midwinter's night or make you coffee when you wake up in the morning. Fish are not great conversationalists. Hmm, then again, neither are some men. Well, of course, a fish can't do what a trouser trout can. Men do have their advantages.

And there's such a wide variety available! Consider the following descriptions of fish and men, and see if you don't recognize a trouser trout you have casted for or landed.

Rainbow (colorful, athletic trout)

The rainbow has character. It hasn't the jewel-like quality of the brook trout, nor the subtle guile of the brown. Rainbows are more like the battery salesman with a chip on his shoulder, daring you to knock it off…. Their behavior is often in the open, up front and honest, and for that reason, fishing for them is often the most fun.

John Merwin, *The New American Trout Fishing*

The fish: Native to the Western United States and a fabulous aerial performer when caught, these hard fighters are full of athleticism and lust for life. They live in the fast waters and usually die younger than other trout, perhaps burned out by their exuberant lifestyle. With a good food supply, they can grow to a sensational size.

The man: Energetic go-getters with an active lifestyle, these trouser trout are often involved in sports, either professionally or recreationally. They may work in an active pursuit ranging from cowboy or construction worker to marine biologist or soldier.

In courtship, they will dazzle a potential mate, but they may put up a fight that can come back to haunt the relationship. They know they're colorful and have a strong streak of vanity. After rainbows become domesticated, they tend to fatten up and start watching people doing on television what they used to do in real life.

Brown (transplanted species, Euro-trout)

This canny foreigner was imported to this continent first from Germany then from Scotland and finally from England…. Of all the varieties of salmon and trout this one is probably the most difficult to catch, for it learns quickly and bites infrequently…. This is a fish that must be approached with caution.

Jeremy Brown and John Power,
The Canadian Fisherman's Handbook

The fish: Brown trout, European natives from Scandinavia to the Mediterranean, were imported to the U.S. East Coast from Germany in the 1880s and have since spread across the country. Browns are hardy fish, but generally more sedentary than their rainbow cousins. They prefer the slow-moving rivers and aggressively guard their territory. Wary and easily spooked, they are hard to catch and tenacious fighters when hooked.

The man: Not necessarily brown, just "not from these parts." They're either from a foreign country or another region within the United States. Given American mobility and the waves of immigrants who formed this country, brown trout are everywhere.

Even if they've lived the same place all their life, they'll often have some charming accent and a stubborn aversion to condoms. They're tenacious about life, striking out into new situations when driven. They can be hard to get to know, but staunchly loyal friends or lovers once won over.

However, they don't adapt very well to sudden changes, tend to have strong opinions about The Way Things Should Be and proudly express their chauvinism.

Golden (rich trout)

The golden trout is the most remote, inaccessible and exclusive of American game fish. He lives only with his own kind…. He exceeds every other trout in flamboyance… The golden is almost invariably a small fish.

Larry Koller, *The Treasury of Angling*

The fish: Exceedingly beautiful and tasty little fish that live in the high altitude streams of the Western United States and Mexico. Relatively small and limited in number, golden trout are highly prized.

The man: Whether earned or inherited, these trouser trout have money…lots of it. F. Scott Fitzgerald wrote that the rich are different from you and me, and in many ways they are. Their wealth may give them access to the finer things in life, or give them fame and power, but even men with lots of money want someone to love.

Their affluence gives them a better bargaining position than the average trout, and cool cash can buy the love they crave in the hottest package available. That doesn't mean this fish is kinder, more generous, smarter or better looking than the average trout. Anglers have been known to overlook an awesome number of flaws to hook and land a golden trout.

Brook (family man trout)

A beautiful, sensitive fish, losing way to civilization but nonetheless an attractive creature revered by many anglers...

Jeremy Brown and John Power,
The Canadian Fisherman's Handbook

The fish: A char salmonid native to the clear, spring-fed streams of the northeastern United States, brook trout are considered the easiest to catch because they can't resist a fly. However, they move in a flash, and you've got to be fast to catch them. Modern industrial society is threatening the habitat and existence of this sensitive fish.

The man: Brookies are family-oriented men who want to have children. If single, they systematically date women to find the mother of their future children, quickly rejecting those who won't do.

If they've had kids and are widowed or divorced with custody, they may be found at Parents Without Partners meetings, looking for the anglers who have a similar mind-set. Some are sensitive New Age guys who share child raising and housekeeping chores, others prefer the chief breadwinner role and make time for their families.

However, just because men produce offspring doesn't automatically make them Brookies. Being a good father requires much more than simply the capacity for spawning.

Salmon (spiritual trout)

He takes deliberately, without the verve and frivolity of a
trout or grayling, but with purpose and power…. Most often
a salmon is a gentleman fighter…. When he sulks, he does
so quietly and with dignity.

Larry Koller, *The Treasury of Angling*

*The fish: Pink-fleshed, big fish distributed throughout
the Northern Hemisphere, salmon variations include Pacific
salmon, Atlantic salmon, sockeye, humpback, chinook,
chum, and coho. Salmon are famous for the effort they
expend to migrate from the ocean to their home spawning
streams – hundreds, even thousands of feet above sea level.
Alaskan Native Americans revere the salmon as a symbol of
well-being.*

The man: Salmon trouser trout are spiritually calm,
rock-solid men who draw their strength from deep internal
sources. Their placid surfaces cover waters that run deep,
and they can have a wild streak which surfaces
unexpectedly. They will go against the flow to fight for
something they believe in.

They may center themselves spiritually through any
number of outlets: church, meditation, perhaps fly-fishing in
the great outdoors. Their spirituality casts a rosy glow over
everyone who knows them. And like smoked salmon, lox,
and nova, they're a treat on Sunday mornings.

Sea trout (salty dogs)

Generally, they take to the sea in search of better feeding
grounds, rather than to fulfill any instinctive urge…. Sea-
runs return to the streams of their origin when it pleases
them.

Larry Koller, *The Treasury of Angling*

The fish: Rainbow, brook, cutthroat, and brown trout have seagoing cousins who head out to the ocean to consume the wide variety of food there and return to native freshwater streams to reproduce. These trout generally grow bigger and feistier than their stream-dwelling relatives.

The man: Sea trout are travelers who may wander when visiting various ports of call. They may be politicians, pilots, entrepreneurs, sailors, or salesmen who are hot to trot when out of town, but still want to return to their gal back home.

Quick-witted fast talkers, they may actually be faithful to their women, but they don't give you that impression when you run into them at trade shows, seminars, and conventions. Salty language and off-color jokes are common among sea trout who run together.

Lake trout (nice guys)

…the world's largest trout and his family's poorest fighter…. For a fish in this weight range he puts up an embarrassingly feeble defense.

Larry Koller, *The Treasury of Angling*

The fish: A member of the char species, lake-grown fish are more sociable with other fish and will travel in schools. With a lake's steady food supply and no current to fight, these trout can grow to enormous proportions.

The man: Lake trout are amiable fellows, the type with whom your mother would like you to hook up. They're pleasant, even-keeled guys who may or may not get your pulse racing, at least not initially.

They're the gentle men that women overlook in their teens and 20s because they're not exciting enough. They're also the kind of men women desperately seek in their late 30s or 40s, when all the men they find available are neurotic Other Fish in the Sea.

Lake trout are upright, honorable, decent men who will be there for you when you need them. Some are also very good cooks, leading the more indulgent of the species to weight problems. Also known as a *mensh* (Yiddish).

Dolly Varden (cross-dressers)

Unfortunately, he is not an outstanding fighter and he suffers a good deal from comparison with other members of the trout family…. In addition, the Dolly for years had an unsavory reputation along coastal waters for feeding on salmon spawn.

Larry Koller, *The Treasury of Angling*

The fish: A Western form of the eastern brook trout or char, Dolly Varden are found in the deep waters of mountain lakes and coastal rivers. The fish was discovered in the 1840s when Charles Dickens' novel Barnaby Rudge *was popular. It is named after the heroine of the book who sported a lavender-spotted dress that matches this trout's coloring. Major meat eaters, they chase other trout.*

The man: While dressing like women doesn't rule these trouser trout out of the heterosexual dating game, it does make a date look like Girls' Night Out. Dolly Vardens are usually more interested in other trout than in female anglers.

Some of the hetero variety dress in manly garb with women's lingerie underneath. Either way, they often have a sense of style, aesthetics, and female empathy that other types of trout don't usually possess.

Whitefish (intellectual trout)

The whitefish is deep and compressed…. It is not an exciting fish to catch and requires some planning for effective execution…. Whitefish does not hit the bait but sort of sucks it in, making it difficult for the fisherman to know when he has a strike.

> Jeremy Brown and John Power,
> *The Canadian Fisherman's Handbook*

The fish: Whitefish are the earliest ancestors of the salmonid species. Slender-bodied and herring-like, with colorless silver scales and deeply-forked tails, they favor deep cold waters in the Northern Hemisphere.

The man: Whitefish are usually too busy with what's going on in their brains to work on a tan. Their considerable intellect may be expressed in words, numbers, art, computer programs, business, law, medicine, or science – almost any mental endeavor.

Often voracious readers, they'll provide ample material for deep and wide-ranging conversations, providing they're not so absorbed in their own thoughts that they don't communicate at all.

Grayling (elder trout)

The grayling is a gentleman adversary…. If a human quality can be ascribed to a fish, the grayling has true *savoir faire.*

> Larry Koller, *The Treasury of Angling*

The fish: Originally found around the Arctic and Northwest Territories, graylings are the second-oldest salmonid after whitefish. Silver-gray, cigar-shaped, with an elegantly flaring dorsal fin, they often give off an aroma of thyme. Graylings are fly-taking, sporting fish, sometimes difficult to fool.

The man: Guys who have lived long enough to go gray or go bald can be graylings, even if those with hair dye it another color. Graylings tell great stories, having experienced the world and heard endless jokes, and they know how to have fun.

While they may not give off an aroma of thyme, they'll often have a collection of after-shaves in their medicine cabinets, gifts from children and grand-children. Charming, mannerly and bon vivant, they sometimes turn sour and become grumpy old men (see Other Fish In The Sea – Carp).

You may find that a combination of two, three or even four types of trout best describe the trouser trout swimming in your life. This is to be expected since most people do not fit neatly into any one category.

There are two other trout types I have identified strictly related to physical characteristics.

Cutthroat (circumcised trout)

Despite the fact that the cutthroat has never been considered a notable fighter, he can leap as well as any rainbow of matching size…. The cutthroat is a true trout, endowed with all the wonderful and exciting characteristics a trout can have.

Larry Koller, *The Treasury of Angling*

The fish: Native trout of the Western United States, distinguished by a trim profile and red throat slash markings on its lower jaw.

The man: Circumcised, which doesn't have any bearing on age, race, personality, intelligence, financial status, or ambition. Circumcision, required in Jewish and Muslim religions, has been a popular practice in the United States, but now the pendulum seems to be swinging in the other direction.

Arguments abound regarding the effects of circumcision on sensitivity, hygiene, appearance, and general usefulness of the practice. However, it is a trout trait that will endure for the foreseeable future.

Steelhead (Mr. Stamina)

Everything you can say about the rainbow doubles when the talk is of steelhead.... Fresh from the sea, he is spirit incarnate of wild waves and rushing rivers.... With your hook fixed to a steelhead you feel the fierceness of these characteristics in his driving runs, his passionate, high jumps to free himself, his rolling and twisting over the leader as his vibrant energy subsides. A battle with a steelhead is a memorable, soul-filling, and often frightening phenomenon.

Larry Koller, *The Treasury of Angling*

The fish: A member of the rainbow family that runs to the sea, these fish have a strong migratory urge to roam far and wide. Native to the Pacific Coast and now found in the Great Lakes region, these trout have great stamina.

The man: Steelhead trout have the staying power to keep going until the angler is satisfied, even if they've reached the end of their spawning cycle. While their perpetual arousal can be a godsend to some women, others may find the endless appetite of steelhead trout to be a burden. If they can't get satisfaction at home, they may develop a migratory urge. His sexual prowess is a powerful lure for anglers who relish a good tussle.

Other Fish in the Sea

"But wait," you say, "These trout are fine-sounding fellows. What about those scum-sucking bottom feeders that make our lives hell? What about those sullen men who were particularly disastrous dates?"

Here's the secret: not all men are trout. Some are Other Fish in the Sea.

While trout represent a man's nobler side, the negative aspects are embodied by Other Fish in the Sea. Unfortunately, there are plenty of these fish to make women miserable, including:

Crabs (unpleasant men)

Guys who have a tough outer shell, protecting their soft defenseless inner selves. Crabs can be hurtful, pinching those closest to them with cynical comments, or just painful to be around because they're angry, resentful or dour. A hermit crab is an onerous combination of crab and clam, both hurtful and inaccessible.

Clams (inaccessible men)

Clams use their hard exterior to hole up inside themselves. They may relax a bit to initially connect with an angler, then shut her out and leave her wondering what went wrong. The harder a woman tries to open a clam, the more fiercely he'll shut down.

Blowfish (egotistical farts)

Blowfish are self-absorbed men who hold the exalted opinion that they are God's gift to women. Inclined to let the world know their opinions, no matter how ill-informed or one-sided, blowfish affect mannerisms of superiority to hide an inferiority complex. Trying to ignore them only makes them more insistent. Men who harass women, on the street or at work, also fall into this category.

Bottom Feeders (abusers)

Detestable fellows who give men a bad reputation, including pedophiles, pornographers, child molesters, rapists, and SOB's who beat women "because they deserve it." They may be alcoholic or have been abused as children, but that's no excuse for treating women and children badly. Also known as *schmucks* (Yiddish), bastards, lowlifes, pricks, creeps.

Eels (slippery smoothies)

Slippery fellows with questionable morals, eels slither out of their commitments, philander on their wives, lie shamelessly, and usually get away with it. They say they'll call, then don't. They'll gloss over your concerns with smooth talk, but their actions reveal their true selves.

Piranhas and Lampreys (predators)

These predators are guys who take advantage of women emotionally, economically, physically, and psychologically. Piranhas are aggressive hit-and-run fish who pounce quickly and go zipping off into the night. Lampreys attach themselves to women and feed off them for as long as they can.

Sea Slugs (couch potatoes)

Sea slugs park on your couch, watch TV, snarf up your snack food and do nothing to enhance the conversation or your life. Slow-moving and dim-witted, land-based slugs have been known to drown themselves in beer. Sprinkling one with salt may generate a quick reaction, but it's best to give a slug the boot before he slimes your entire life.

Urchins (helpless invertebrates)

Fellows who want you to pluck them off the shelf. They'll wave their tentacles seductively, but once you pick them up, they don't do much. They may give you a nasty sting if you handle them roughly. Urchins are prone to depression and will expect you to cheer them up.

Octopus (smothering invertebrates)

An octopus gradually insinuates himself into the world of the women he meets, and gloms on with his sucker-studded personality. Once established, he slowly kills whatever liveliness existed before he came on the scene.

Flying Fish (manic maniacs)

Guys who unpredictably swing between emotional and energy highs and lows. They'll seem reasonably normal, then suddenly they'll move all the furniture around at 3 a.m., babbling about the novel they're going to write. Or they'll abruptly get cold, distant, and depressed, and there's no obvious reason why. They may be like Dr. Jekyll and Mr. Hyde: charming and caring at tea time, raging maniacs after dinner. Have a little sympathy. It's not something they do intentionally, unless they refuse to take their prescribed medications.

Carp (constant complainers)

Guys who are never happy with the way things are and let you know it. Not to be confused with a flying fish on a down cycle, they've got to complain about something, and everything is a target for their acid tongues. Carp can also be major-league whiners who make guilt-provoking accusations as they moan and sigh about everything they don't like.

Clown Fish (colorful critics)

This fish is colorful, showy, often funny, but he's armed with a poisonous sense of humor. They use their wit to be the center of attention, making people laugh while they deliver stinging critiques and put-downs.

Trash Fish (generally unacceptable)

Men with inadequate personal hygiene, poor table manners, excessive sloppiness, rude behavior, profuse profanity and general obtuseness. Trash fish come in many forms in every stream. Anglers have to reel in so many trash fish before netting a trout, resulting in a high frogs-to-princes ratio – as in "You've got to kiss a lot of" the former before you find the latter.

Comparing the men in your life to the above descriptions, you will no doubt find some of our otherwise noble trout may have a few characteristics of these Other Fish in the Sea. The combinations are endless.

For example, brown trout, with their strong opinions, can easily become blowfish. Brilliant whitefish can sometimes be crabs. Passive lake trout can be transformed into urchins. And any kind of trout can become flying fish or carp.

Although no one will precisely fit any particular category, if the men you know exhibit few traits associated with trout and more associated with Other Fish in the Sea, I recommend serious reconsideration of those relationships.

Quiz: Trout or Other Fish in the Sea?

This quiz is designed to help you determine where the men in your life land in the spectrum of True Noble Trout versus Other Fish in the Sea. If possible, get your guy to take the quiz with you.

Select one reply for each statement. A scoring key at the end gives the numerical value for each answer. After adding up the total, look up the category he most closely resembles.

1. When the two of you go somewhere in the car, he opens the door for you:
a. almost every time.
b. if you're dressed up for a special date.
c. only when you've got your hands full or ask him.
d. infrequently.
e. if he's got you bound and gagged.

2. He feels like spawning but you aren't in the mood. He:
a. suggests a sensuous activity like a massage or a soak in the hot tub.
b. snuggles for a while to see if he can arouse you.
c. pulls out his collection of girlie magazines and goes off to satisfy himself.
d. gets all huffy and goes off to sulk.
e. goes ahead and does what he damn well pleases.

3. When driving somewhere you've never been before, he:
a. thinks ahead and gets specific directions.
b. takes a map and tries to figure it out as you go.
c. gets to the general vicinity and asks for directions only as a last resort.

d. tosses a pile of maps in your lap and tells you to get busy.
e. drives around until the destination magically appears.

4. He has a choice of two free tickets to a sporting event, a movie or an outdoor cultural festival. He:
a. discusses the most appealing option with you.
b. calls up a buddy and invites him to the sporting event.
c. does what most appeals to him without consulting you.
d. tries to get free tickets for all three events.
e. takes another woman to the event of her choice.

5. In the bathroom, he leaves the toilet seat:
a. lid closed, seat down.
b. lid up, seat down.
c. seat up.
d. up or down, depends what he did there last.
e. sprinkled with yellow spots.

6. He's just been out with you for the first time, and you enjoyed each other's company (no sex was involved). He says he'll call and he:
a. calls the next day to say thanks and suggest another date.
b. calls within one to two days to ask how things are going.
c. calls after a week has gone by.
d. never calls again.
e. starts making obscene phone calls to you in the middle of the night.

7. He runs up a $300 phone bill while living at your place, gets laid off, and can't pay you back immediately. He:
a. borrows from his credit card and pays you back in full all at once.
b. pays you back in full on an agreed-to schedule.
c. makes a few payments and stops when money gets too tight.

d. gives you something he thinks is the equivalent of what he owes, such as his record album collection.
e. moves to another state, declares bankruptcy and puts you down as a creditor.

8. You have both had a rough day at work. You want to talk and all he wants to do is blast monsters on his computer to unwind. He:
a. sympathetically listens to you unload about your day, then goes to blow up monsters for both of you.
b. says, "I've gotta kill some demons. I'll be back."
c. grabs a beer and turns on the computer without saying anything.
d. says, "Can't you see I'm busy? Leave me alone."
e. grabs a real gun and starts shooting up the place.

9. He's been asked to represent his business in a meeting with the city council. Surveying his wardrobe, he selects:
a. a dark suit, well-pressed shirt, understated tie (his best GQ look).
b. a sport coat, khaki pants, cartoon character tie (his usual office attire).
c. a black leather jacket, black T-shirt, black jeans (his in-charge look).
d. whatever clothing he can find without a large rip or stain.
e. a T-shirt with a rude slogan and athletic shorts.

10. He's decided that the six-month relationship you've been having isn't living up to his expectations or hopes. He:
a. initiates a discussion about "the relationship."
b. initiates an argument about "the relationship."
c. clams up and watches TV.
d. leaves without warning.
e. mails you a photo of himself and another woman at the beach with a note saying "The weather is great, glad you're not here."

11. Someone asks him about the culture of tuna fishing in Japan, a subject about which he knows next to nothing. He:
a. admits to knowing very little on the topic and suggests other resources.
b. states he's not an expert and hazards a guess.
c. talks about Japanese food, automobiles, stereo equipment.
d. says, "Sorry Charlie, we don't want tunas with good taste, we want tunas that taste good."
e. holds forth with gusto on the topic.

12. He's invited a small group of friends over for a casual dinner. He serves:
a. fresh grilled salmon, spinach salad, potatoes au gratin, fruit and cheese for dessert, served with a top-rated Chardonnay from his extensive wine collection.
b. baked chicken breasts, chopped frozen spinach, baked potatoes, ice cream for dessert, served with white table wine.
c. frozen fish sticks, canned peas, Tater Tots (baked with the fish sticks), Oreos for dessert, served with cold beer.
d. carry out Chinese food, right out of the carton, with the fortune cookies for dessert, served with cheap tequila.
e. A beer, and announces it's potluck.

13. To celebrate a significant anniversary, he's inclined to select the following kind of gift:
a. extravagant and substantial, like good jewelry or an exotic vacation.
b. thoughtful yet affordable, like flowers, chocolate, champagne, dinner at a nice restaurant.
c. practical, like a garage door opener or garbage disposal.
d. selfish, like power tools.
e. perfect, like a one-way ticket to Tahiti for himself.

Scoring

a = 4 points   b = 3 points   c = 2 points
d = 1 point   e = 0 points

42 - 52 points: True Noble Trout. He is a considerate, caring person who's aware of others' feelings and needs. He gets an "A" for chivalry. No matter what type of trout, an angler would be glad to know him, at least as a friend. Does he have a brother?

32 - 41 points: Good Quality Trout. He has many positive aspects of the True Noble Trout's characteristics, with a bit of immaturity, machismo, and/or self-centeredness coloring an otherwise great nature. He's still a good catch.

21 - 31 points: Fishy Pseudo-Trout. He has some redeeming qualities, but lacks awareness of social propriety and others' needs and feelings. In such relationships, an angler will find plenty of things to make fun of when she's discussing the fishing with her girlfriends.

14 - 20 points: True Other Fish in the Sea. He is the center of his universe and anyone who associates with him must submit to his interpretation of the rules. You call that a relationship?

0 - 13 points: Either he is a psychopath or did not take this quiz seriously. It's just not a guy thing to do.

Chapter Three

The Compleat Angler:
Natural, Artificial and Exotic Lures

Margo examined her appearance in the ladies room mirror. Her short red hair fluffed appealingly. Not too much make-up, just enough to spark her hazel eyes and accentuate her full lips.

She fiddled with her intricate treasure necklace, a collection of beads and charms that tinkled of their own accord.

She adjusted her skirt, which was short enough to show off her long legs without screaming "Whore here!" Satisfied everything was in place, she sauntered into the nightclub.

Scanning the room for men not already engrossed in co-ed conversation, Margo spotted a likely candidate. She parked herself at the bar, next to a beefy blonde fellow with owlish glasses.

His eyes were immediately drawn to her chest, not because she was amply endowed or possessed perky nipples.

"Wow, that's a very interesting necklace," he said.

"Why, thank you," said Margo. "I found it at a funky little boutique in Baltimore. Ever been to Fells Point?"

As they launched into their conversation, Margo thought to herself, "The interesting jewelry does it every time."

*   *   *

Gail Rubin

The Art of Luring Trout

The whole question of what trout think they are looking at
when they watch a dry fly float toward them is
unanswerable. Since trout probably do not think at all, let's
rephrase the question. What is it about a floating artificial
fly that stimulates the trout to respond by eating it?

M.R. Montgomery, *The Way of the Trout*

Izaak Walton thought trout bit on lures more out of
wantonness than hunger. Still, the most effective way to
catch fish is to feed them what they like. Trout fish like
eating insects, spiders, small fish, and other creepy-crawly
things that fall in the water. That's why the sport is called
fly-fishing. It would be quite rare for a trout to bite on an
imitation vegetable lure, although they have been known to
eat cheese balls and bread.

Trout hunt by sight, and trouser trout are attracted by
looks first, such as a woman's shape, how she dresses and
presents herself. Snagging a trouser trout by personality
alone would be the equivalent of catching a fish by willing
it out of the water and into your landing net. If you could do
that, you wouldn't be reading this book, would you?

Although you don't have to be a stellar beauty to hook a
trouser trout, good looks do make the job much easier.
Hence, women's magazines offer an endless stream of
beauty tips regarding weight, body fat, exercises, makeup
application, hair styling, wardrobe selection, and wrinkle
reduction. After looking at these magazines filled with
unreal images of beauty, most women of average build and
looks feel shapeless, ugly and old.

These magazines don't usually tell you personality goes
a long way to compensate for ordinary looks. Your self-
confidence doesn't help a magazine sell their advertisers'
products. A positive outlook, genuine smile, interest in the
world around you, and basic physical fitness is appreciated

by the opposite sex more than you may realize…
particularly by a trout who's hooked by more than just
looks.

Still, any prepared angler will have lures – trouser trout
flies, if you will – in her tackle box. These attention-getters
are designed to simply encourage a strike. Setting the hook
and reeling him in depends on your finely tuned
interpersonal skills.

Seasonal Lures and Unusual Names

It is reasonable that you should know with what baits you
must angle for every kind of fish in each month of the year,
which is the gist of the art. And unless these baits are well
known by you, all your other skill hitherto avails little to
your purpose.

Dame Juliana Berners,
The Treatise of Fishing with an Angle

In the 1400s, Dame Juliana Berners made her flies out
of wool, leather, fur, silk, and feathers, and each kind of lure
had a specific season for its use. Similarly, today's trouser
trout anglers create lures from the very same materials, in
addition to the plethora of synthetics that did not exist in
Dame Juliana's time. Every season has its special lures,
depending on climate.

An angler in a four-season climate might sport a
cashmere sweater in winter, a sheer silk blouse in spring, a
gauzy cotton dress in summer and a snappy leather jacket in
the fall. Those in warmer climates forgo wool and leather
for lighter materials year-round, and they can wear bathing
suits outdoors much more frequently than someone in
Buffalo, New York.

No matter what the temperature or time of year,
intelligence, wit and empathy are never out of season.
However, these qualities won't lure the quarry if he's

stupid, humorless or self-centered. You don't really want that kind of catch, anyway. So don't be despondent if your sharp mind and sweet nature aren't drawing him in. He doesn't deserve you.

There are about 25,000 recognized artificial fly patterns in the trout fishing world, although there is no official organization that determines what constitutes a recognized fly pattern. If you listen to anglers talk about these flies, unless you are as passionate about fishing as they are, your eyes will glaze over.

There are some mighty amusing names for these lures, some of which are highly revered in fishing circles. Making fun of the names Adams, Wulff, Orvis and any kind of caddis, hopper, or mayfly is done at your own peril.

Still, you have to smile about whole classes of Woolly Buggers, Humpies (including the Yellow Humpy or Goofus Bug), Zonkers, Nobblers, Boobies, and Damsels.

Individual lures have names such as the Butcher Nymph, Pink Deviant, Bread Crust, Sofa Pillow, Dinky Purple-Breasted Sedge, Pink Panther, Hairy Prince Green Butt, the Waggy, Zug Bug, Vindaloo, Zulu, and the revered Royal Coachman.

When an angler has a trouser trout on the line, the nicknames he calls her can sound a lot like lures. A few great angler aliases: Big Mama, Darlin', Peaches, Princess, Sunshine, Sweetie Pie, Toots, and my personal favorite, the Wild Wahini.

Presentation

The art of proper presentation – what gets revealed, what stays hidden, what goes with what – can make or break an angler's success. While a costume party may be apropos for outrageous couture, regularly wearing outlandish outfits does not attract trout. Don't become a fashion fatality. Dress with care.

The successful angler assembles outfits that will make a man notice and draw him from across the room, not send him screaming for the exit as you approach. Clothing is an incredibly important trouser trout lure with many variables to consider. Here are a few fashion tips to take to heart.

• Don't mix patterns. Even when fashion industry mavens say it's okay to wear a combination of florals, stripes, paisleys, squares, and plaids, don't believe them. They've gone temporarily insane full-time. Stick with one pattern combined with solid colors.

• Avoid plaid suits. Plaid skirts are acceptable. Only those of the Celtic persuasion who can identify the family tartan should indulge in any greater amount of plaid coverage.

• Shun Spandex outside the gym unless you are in tip-top shape. If you are Ms. Muscles, flaunt it, baby.

• Wear suitable underwear. If you are Caucasian, don't wear a dark bra under a light shirt. Dark foundation wear is preferable for dark-skinned women. Beware of wandering bra straps that show themselves. Get rid of panties and bras that need constant tugging.

• Keep clean. Don't deliberately wear clothes that are stained, torn or smelly when trouser trout angling. However, it is acceptable, sometimes even attractive, to get down and dirty while gardening, camping, hiking and other great outdoors undertakings.

• If you can carry it off, try out different looks. From sultry siren to bookish intellectual, or Annie Hall to Annie Oakley, theme dressing can help you match the hatch.

Matching the Hatch

Fly fishermen pride themselves on being able to determine what insects the fish are eating at a particular moment and matching whatever's hatching with an artificial fly. The "match-the-hatch" theory suggests if you present something that looks like what the fish are already eating, you've got a much better chance of getting a strike.

In trouser trout angling, you match the hatch with specific lures and actions timed to hook the type of trout being sought. For example, if you're after a rainbow, engage in endeavors such as swimming or tennis while wearing your most fetching athletic gear. Seeking salmon? Go to church or volunteer for some worthy cause in modest garb. Pursue whitefish in a university class or your favorite bookstore wearing jeans and blazer.

Ideally, you pursue such activities because you have a genuine interest in them, not just in the hopes of landing a trout. Matching the hatch outside of your own interests will result in frustration down the road. You'll want to go camping in the woods and he'll want to go camping in a nice hotel. Eventually you'll look at each other and ponder, "What was I thinking?"

You can also match the hatch by projecting a particular image, after identifying interests of the trout that intrigue you. If you want to lasso a cowboy, dress like a rodeo queen. For fishing during business hours, pull out that power suit and look like you're in charge. A classy golden trout is more likely to recognize you as a tango partner if you're wearing a zesty little black dress, and he may mistake you for the hired help if you're in overalls.

Whatever your style of dressing, it's important to dress the way that makes you feel your best and expresses your own identity. An outfit that makes you feel snappy doesn't have to be dressy. It's a combination of color, style and comfort that lets your true spirit shine through and broadcast to the world "This Is Me!"

Attractor Colors

In fishing, attractors are flashy lures that attract the fish's attention because they're big and bright in eye-popping colors. To the fish underwater, the colors look muted and the form may resemble something a trout would actually eat. Even though they don't imitate specific life forms, attractors will prompt a fish to strike with abandon.

Humans are almost the only species on earth in which the female presents herself more colorfully than the male. For trouser trout anglers, the right colors in clothing and accessories serve as powerful attractors.

You may have sneered at the concept of learning your colors, but trust me, it works amazingly well. Dressed in the wrong colors, an otherwise perky angler becomes drab, lifeless and invisible. While dressed in the right colors, she crackles with energy and magnetism, and people will notice.

Personally, as a dark brunette with pale skin, I know for a fact that pastels and browns make me feel frumpy and look ill. But when dressed in crisp, bright colors or black and white, I'm ready to tackle anything!

The energy and enthusiasm you can get from wearing your correct colors, beyond their function as an attractor lure, make them well worth learning. Put attractor colors to work for you and you'll be amazed at their drawing power.

The book *Color Me Beautiful* provides helpful guidelines to determine your personal color category, described as a season. Author Carole Jackson shows how your skin tone, hair and eye color determine what colors look best on you. Here's a quick sketch of the seasons and their colors:

Winters sparkle in clear, vivid, cool colors with blue undertones, black, white, navy, shades of gray and bright primary colors.

Summers shine in soft colors with blue undertones, shades of blue and rose, lavender, plum and pastels.

Autumns glow in warm colors with golden undertones, like brown, beige, orange, gold and shades of green.

Springs shimmer in peachy and golden colors with yellow undertones, clear warm colors like bright blues, yellow and pink.

Hardware

Margo's example at the start of this chapter shows that interesting jewelry does yeoman's work to attract attention and start conversations. Cost is unimportant, as long as the jewelry is visually intriguing and has an engaging story behind it. Hand-crafted ornamentation with beads, glass, ceramics, and unusual metal objects will generally attract more attention than classic silver or gold accents.

Other good conversation-sparking candidates are Native American silver and semi-precious stone inlaid pieces, African beads, and pieces composed of various trinkets. If you're after a classy look, by all means don the pearls or elegant gemstone jewelry. Necklaces and brooches will call attention to your chest, bracelets and rings to your hands, and earrings to your face.

Nose rings, eyebrow studs and other facial jewelry will generally work against all but the youngest anglers. Pierced body parts besides a few holes in the earlobes will attract similarly decorated guys. If that's the type of trout you want to attract, pierce away! Throw in a few visible tattoos for good measure.

Just don't expect any sympathy if you go crying to anyone when you reach middle age and realize what a fool you've been. Some of those holes may heal up, and some may not. Certainly the tattoos will last a long time, and if you have them removed, you'll have some lovely scars to remember them by.

Hair and Makeup

Well-kept hair and appropriate makeup work incredibly well as trouser trout lures. For evidence of their effectiveness, peruse the pages of any women's magazine, where cosmetics and hair care products comprise a big chunk of the companies advertising to garner your hard-earned dollars.

Hair and makeup is the mainstay of actors and performers, creating the looks that get burned into the public's consciousness. The show doesn't go on until the makeup does.

We all know makeup can go a long way to enhance your looks – most of the time. With the right touch, a face that blends in with the crowd will stand out. Catch that trout's eye and you're not far from getting a strike.

Beware, though, of a heavy hand with the powder and paint. Too much makeup makes you a caricature of a beautiful woman. Remember, clowns use makeup, too.

Many trouser trout think long hair is sexy, and given the choice will go for an angler with long hair before considering the woman with a shorter 'do.

However, men don't have to spend all that precious time every day blow-drying, curling and styling flowing tresses. Unless you really enjoy having long hair and the attendant exertions to keep your mane looking good, do yourself a favor and cut it short.

There are plenty of women who demonstrate that you can have short hair and a long line of lunkers – Gwyneth Paltrow, Jamie Lee Curtis, Isabella Rossellini, and Carmen Diaz come to mind.

Long hair *is* an incredible lure. I once had the experience of modeling for a press kit on hair extensions. In one afternoon, I exchanged short, perky, straight hair for a shoulder-length mane of dark curls. On the way home from the salon, I stopped in the grocery store to pick up a few items.

As I strolled down the aisle, tossing my head to test the unfamiliar feeling of long hair, men were literally stopping and staring after me. Out of the corner of my eye, I spied a fellow who backed up his cart to get another look. With my short hair, men didn't stare much, let alone do double takes.

I met a most charming Frenchman while I had my artificially long hair. He was most dismayed when the extensions came out.

Long or short, keep your hair in good trim and wash it regularly. Stringy, dirty, unkempt hair is a major trouser trout repellent. Here's a handy hint from Large Animal Land: Mane N' Tail Conditioner, originally formulated for horses, fabulously conditions human hair, giving it body and shine beyond other hair care products I've tried.

Does she or doesn't she? Most trout don't care or want to know about hair coloring. If you're an older angler and gray hair makes you feel out of the game, by all means color your hair a reasonable shade. Just don't overdo it and become a member of the Screaming Orange Spinsters or the Blue-Haired Old Ladies' Club.

Fancy Footwear

Good footwear is an important piece of equipment in trouser trout angling. My brother the Dolly Varden says, "The higher the heel, the quicker the reel."

He has a point. There's a reason Frederick's of Hollywood carries shoes and boots with five- and six-inch heels to complement their notorious outfits. Trouser trout find such footwear incredibly sexy – but trout don't have to wear them.

I find even three-inch heels to be incredible torture devices. How can an angler concentrate on her leader lines when her feet and back hurt and she's worried about twisting her ankle? My advice: get yourself some outrageous cowboy boots. We're not talking about boring ropers or real work boots, but bright, multi-colored, pointy-toed creations.

Cowboy boots combine comfort and style in one great package that gets attention, starts conversations and makes you feel pretty darned sparky. In good cowboy boots, you can stand all day, dance all night, and still be smiling as you reel in your trout *du jour*.

Good sources include respected boot manufacturers like Nocona, Justin, Lucchese and Tony Lama, makers of stylin' high-quality footwear, as well as smaller companies like Rocketbuster. There are also many individual boot makers who produce incredible handmade leather wonders.

One does not need to be the Imelda Marcos of cowboy boots. With proper care, one good pair of boots lasts a very long time, and they just get more comfortable with age. I personally have 13 pair, which is more than most people desire or need, but I build outfits around my boots.

Unless you've got the treasury of the Philippines at your disposal, finances may limit your collection. A decent pair of boots can cost anywhere from $200 to $600, and really fancy ones can cost thousands, depending on the detail involved. I've got a few thousand dollars invested in my cowboy boot collection. Gee, maybe I am the Imelda Marcos of cowboy boots.

Still, buying quality boots is well worthwhile because of the longwearing comfort and timeless style they provide.

Lingerie Lures

When fishing for trout, you may endure certain discomforts, such as mosquitoes, sunburn, wet clothes, cold hands and feet. Similarly, when angling for trouser trout, you tolerate some discomfort if the lure is effective. Such is the case with lingerie.

Gail Rubin

While garters are sexy, those little clips that hold the stockings can really dig into the back of your legs. Satin and lace bustiers gouge your rib cage, fishnet stockings impress patterns on your legs, and barely-there thongs give you a perpetual wedgie. Fortunately, most women don't have to wear these items more than a few hours. Often, they'll come off soon after they're revealed.

Those underthings designed for all-day augmentation – The Wonder Bra, with its cleavage-enhancing properties, shapers, formerly known as girdles, and support panty hose – help make a less-than-perfect body look good, but are not particularly comfortable.

Whatever advantage they provide in shapeliness may be negated by a perpetually pained look hearkening back to the dour expressions of women in turn-of-the-century portraits (no doubt prompted by their tight corsets and domineering trout). Still, many well-endowed anglers find these undergarments provide blessed support under the pull of gravity.

Happily, not all sexy lingerie is uncomfortable. Silk camisoles and shorts, satiny nightshirts, even clingy cotton tank tops feel and look good to both angler and trout. Well-fitting, flattering undergarments let an angler feel superb while looking her best.

Synthetic Lures

One advantage modern trouser trout anglers have over our predecessors is synthetic materials – plastics and plastic surgery. Artificial enhancements can provide hefty breasts, a trim tummy and a curvy tush by bodily carving or implanting those attractors that previous generations used corsets to achieve. Wrinkles, bags and droops can be smoothed away, eyes opened wide, thin lips plumped, and overwhelming noses reduced.

Synthetic lures are useful to encourage what's called big-egg behavior – a magnetic response to larger-than-normal attractors, a phenomenon that occurs in many wildlife species.

As M.R. Montgomery noted in *The Way of the Trout*, "The human being is not above this sort of thing, as evidenced by the behavior of some of us when confronted with secondary sexual characteristics of the gigantic sort. Not only big bosoms but big eyes are somehow more attractive to men than merely functional ones."

Many, many women have succumbed to the siren song of the plastic surgeon. My opinion: artificially enhancing one's chest with implants is stupid. More than 440,000 women who have suffered as a result of their implants participated in a 1994 class-action lawsuit against five manufacturers.

These women suffered symptoms that included fatigue, muscle aches and spasms, nausea, sinusitis, depression, chronic pain, severe hardening of the breasts at the implant site, loss of sensation, joint pain, tingling in the limbs, night sweats, hair loss, rheumatoid arthritis, and other unpleasant physical malfunctions.

I can understand women who want implants as replacement after breast cancer surgery. I am less sympathetic toward anglers who augment two functional, if smaller-than-desired breasts. Even with improvements in implant technology, the pursuit of cleavage is not worth the risks of implants. If you feel "you must, you must, you must increase the bust," get some falsies and stuff your bra.

Live Bait

Using live bait in fishing often improves the chances of landing a catch. This is also true in trouser trout angling. Dogs are one of the best types of live bait for attracting the attention of a potential lunker.

When you have a dog, you get out for walks on a regular basis, which is good for your health as well as for casting practice. A frisky dog with an attractive personality gives a guy a good excuse to talk to you. If he's got a dog, it gives you an excuse to talk to him.

If you both have dogs, they will no doubt try to sniff each other's genitals, giving you an excuse to toss a harmless leader line about dog manners, something like, "I've always thought that was a great way to get to know someone."

You can casually determine if he often visits that particular park, and perhaps he'll make a mental note to return. You'll know you share a love of dogs, maybe you've got some other interests in common.

Big friendly dogs like Labrador retrievers or basset hounds are better companions for striking up casual conversations than small high-strung dogs like terriers. If you have to yell at your pooch in a vain attempt to calm it down while chatting with a lunker, it's like having unruly children come along on a first date.

You can also take exotic pets for a walk to get interesting results. A cat on a leash attracts much more attention than any old dog, but you'll need a good story to go with it ("I have to get her out of the house occasionally or she consumes tortilla chips while my back is turned."). One friend of mine ventures out with a pet parrot or cockatiel perched on her head or shoulder – always a sure-fire conversation starter.

Culinary Lures

Is the way to a man's heart through his stomach?

Absolutely! Trout have voracious appetites that demand to be fed.

Many modern guys have cultivated cooking skills, but the times haven't changed so much that a man doesn't appreciate a delicious home-cooked meal made by someone else. And there are still plenty of trout that can't cook worth a darn.

The lure of being a good cook is not obvious, unless you meet at a potluck party and can point out the fine dish that you meticulously prepared. You can make sure to bring your culinary prowess up early in the conversation, but beware of tossing out fancy French food terms unless you know the correct pronunciation. He might know more than you do.

Inviting a trouser trout for a home-cooked meal is a very intimate overture. Make sure he's someone you want to know better first, because he's going to be in your home.

Keep the menu simple, with minimal requirements for last-minute preparations. You don't want a crazed demeanor while juggling several complicated dishes detracting attention from your stellar self or the food.

As any home economics teacher can tell you, successful home entertaining requires more than just cooking skills. Your domicile must be clean, the table set, appropriate background music selected. Even a casual get-together involves some planning and preparation. If you're not up for it, go out to eat.

Even if you're not having him over for dinner, keep your refrigerator and pantry stocked with at least the basics for entertaining – some decent beer or wine, soda, some fruit and cheese, easily prepared comestibles. It's nice to linger together over a little snack if the evening's going well.

If you land a trout who can cook, bravo! Mealtimes can be a fun shared activity. *Bon appetit!*

Conversational Lures

When you can catch a trout's eye by catching his ear, you are a good conversationalist. Being a good conversationalist is more than expressing yourself verbally, it's being able to listen well.

If you're shy and uncomfortable about speaking up, don't worry! A lot of guys are more than willing to fill up empty conversational spaces talking about themselves. If he's shy and needs some encouragement to talk, it is easy to get a conversation flowing.

The keys to being a good conversationalist are similar to successful angling skills: observing the stream, blending your lure into the natural environment, and keeping connected with the fish once he's on the line.

In conversation, this translates to:

• Make eye contact while talking and listening.
• Pay attention to what he is saying.
• Avoid interrupting – if he doesn't finish his sentence before you start talking, you're interrupting.
• Ask questions rather than make statements. You'll get to talk about yourself in due course.

If a guy doesn't give you the opportunity to talk about yourself, chances are he's a blowfish. Sea trout, talkative as they are, know when to shut up and listen. The border between a trout and an Other Fish in the Sea rests on such very fine lines.

Chapter Four

Where the Lunkers Lurk:
Trouser Trout Habitat

A my sighed as she scanned the crowded ballroom at the
Sheraton. God, she hated these singles mixers
sponsored by the local synagogues. She thought, "Why does
a smart, pretty, professional woman subject herself to this
ordeal?"

The energy in the room was driven by desperate men
and women who circulated with their mothers' voices
ringing in their brains, egging them on to find some nice
Jewish boy or girl.

Amy was chumming with Margo and Helen. Her
girlfriends, not Jewish, were indifferent to religious
preferences and didn't mind trying to land a good catch at
an event billed for Jewish singles.

They'd come to the dance together, then split up to troll
different parts of the room. So far, Amy had hooked an
internist ("A doctor, that's good!" says Mom), an Israeli
("Oy, they're so aggressive"), and a paralegal with a cute
smile ("What, not a lawyer?").

Midway through the event, they compared their
progress. Margo had met an environmental scientist and a
writer who worked for a trade association, while Helen had
a securities broker and a computer programmer on the line.
They all agreed that none of these guys were terribly
compelling, but they were there to meet men, so they
bravely plunged back into the crowd, hoping to find Mr.
Right.

Lord, Amy hated these meat markets. Well, if the
evening's catch turned out to be a blue plate special of

Other Fish in the Sea, at least she knew they were all cutthroats.

* * *

Where and When to Fish

If you want to catch a trout, don't fish in a herring barrel.
Jewish Grandmother Proverb

What is wrong with this picture?

In fishing terms, the anglers at the dance are going for quantity over quality under time pressure, and it does not make for a fun fishing trip. The point of this singles dance is to MEET MEN (or, on the other side of the gender fence, meet women), as many as you can in the few hours of the event.

"How many can I catch?" "Will they be lunkers or losers?" "How will I know since I can hardly hear what they're saying because the music is so loud?" These thoughts put great pressure on everyone involved.

While the new phenomenon of speed dating combines quantity, speed and time limits, the format eliminates the rejection fear factor. At a dance, if he's interested and you're not, extrication can be awkward.

Many singles dances have more emphasis on "single" rather than "dancing," making what could otherwise be a fun evening into a joyless campaign to connect with someone you might possibly be interested in, but probably not. There are better ways to land a lunker.

Some of us are city gals, while others prefer the country. But whether you navigate concrete canyons or wide-open spaces, there are plenty of trouser trout waiting to make your acquaintance. The places one fishes are as important as the trout you're after. The trick is to fish the right streams when the trout are biting.

50

Trouser trout angling is always in season. Although you can go fishing any time of year, it's especially compelling during the lusty month of May. When warm springtime weather gets the insects flying and the hormones circulating, all types of anglers head for the streams, which can be in the park, the gym, the library, a local café, and other places.

Continuing through the seasons, so many personal ads favor beach walks, we must use summer romances to reactivate our primeval connection to the ocean. The crisp days and nights of autumn call us out to frolic in the woods and snuggle up to someone warm. Winter conjures up images of cozy fireside interludes with a charming lunker and a bottle of wine.

But where do we go to find these trout? Fishing texts are loaded with diagrams of streams, mapping rocks "A," "B," "C," and "D," indicating where a trout would most likely abide. If only trouser trout fishing spots were as easy to diagram in real life!

In fact, the noble trouser trout abides in hidden places that are right in front of our noses. Here are some guidelines to point you toward the noble trouser trout and help you to avoid those Other Fish in the Sea.

Quality Streams

Finding trout is the most important key in catching them. Consistently finding trout means understanding how the trout themselves behave, how they interact with their stream environment, and how they interact with – or, more properly, react to – fishermen.

John Merwin, *The New American Trout Fishing*

In the dance of angler and trout, do what you like and the fish will follow. Trout fishing has its blue-ribbon waters, rivers like the Blackfoot, the Madison, the San Juan, and the

Battenkill. In trouser trout angling, quality streams are the good places to meet quality men. Some of these places may have been recommended by your mother.

If you like to dance, go to dances or dance lessons. There are plenty of other dance opportunities besides the "singles" variety. You'll find all sorts of different trout populating swing dances, country western clubs, folk dances, contra dances, tango soirees, square dances and more. You're likely to find athletic rainbow trout, graylings and perhaps a few golden trout in these streams.

If you like to camp or hike but don't have buddies to go with, join the Sierra Club or other outdoor groups – some are remarkable trout markets. Many universities and colleges offer low-cost extension classes that combine learning with a great outdoor experience. Some even organize trips just for fun. The outdoorsy rainbow, some brown trout, whitefish, and salmon are likely candidates here.

If you like popular science, check out the local astronomy club. Star parties provide a great excuse to get close to a man in the dark ("Ooh, let me look in that telescope!"). Computer user group meetings bring all sorts of smart folks together.

Archeology, zoology, biology, all the scientific fields hold opportunities for learning and meeting a good catch. The intellectual whitefish and the nice guy lake trout are likely lurking in these streams.

If you've got a spiritual nature, attend a church, synagogue, mosque, or whatever suits your religious leaning. You could hook a trout for a match made in heaven with a salmon, lake trout, or cutthroat.

At the very least, you'll get a break from your busy schedule to relax and gain some valuable perspective reflecting on life. An attitude of gratitude can really lift your spirits, and may clarify your vision.

Go out and learn something! Learn to play guitar in a group, take art or history lessons, sharpen your business skills, or perhaps indulge in a wine appreciation class.

In addition to learning something new, you may also experience personal growth and insights, a nice by-product of taking a class. You'll find whitefish galore, and many other types of trout, depending on the kind of class you take.

Join a club or volunteer with any kind of organization that brings people of common interests together. There are clubs and organizations devoted to just about any activity you'd care to name, and coed groups are good for meeting all kinds of trout.

Professional organizations are rich with brown trout, sea trout and whitefish, even golden trout. Parents Without Partners can be loaded with brookies. The YMCA or health clubs are a good source for rainbows or any type of trout concerned about staying in shape.

Don't overlook the connections that friends and co-workers can provide. Your friends won't deliberately steer you wrong, if they are indeed true friends. And your co-workers have no reason to hook you up with an Other Fish in the Sea, unless you've been a jerk on the job.

By going to places to do things *you* like to do, you're likely find a similarly inclined trout. Bingo! You can hook up because you have something in common. In doing *whatever* we enjoy, we find others who enjoy it too. Chances are you'd probably enjoy doing whatever it is together.

As my mother said, there are plenty of fish in the sea. And there *are* tons of available men out there. However, you won't have much in common with a lot of them. The interesting ones you can lure are rare; the ones you may actually want to land are scarce.

However, by doing things that are right for you and your target trout, it becomes more likely he will someday be swimming by your side.

The truth is, you never know where you might successfully hook a trouser trout. In the course of my long and varied angling career, I've snagged trouser trout while standing in line at the post office, using the office photocopier, and riding public transportation. Some trouser trout will strike if you exhibit the slightest interest in them, so anglers, be alert at all times.

Of course, you also run the risk of finding Other Fish in the Sea in any quality stream. Blowfish, those egotistical farts, and trash fish seem to be especially populous and show up everywhere.

A fellow who seems to be a trout generally won't show his Other Fish tendencies until you've been around him for a while and he's no longer on his best behavior. So, quality streams don't guarantee you'll net a trout, but your chances are much better than in the stock-and-pull streams.

Stock and Pull Streams

Modern-day, fast-paced living does not allow the catch-as-catch-can angler enough time to travel to distant waters seeking top-notch fishing.

Howard Brant, *How To Catch Trout*

In the fishing world, a stock and pull stream is regularly replenished with dim-witted hatchery-raised fish that are just as frequently pulled out by fishermen. For trouser trout angling, stock and pull streams are the obvious places that are likely to hold less-than-stellar trout, or worse, bottom feeders. But just as you find Other Fish in the Sea in quality streams, you can find trout in stock and pull streams. Stock and pull streams include these following places.

Bars – At any type of bar, the only thing you can assume about the guys there is that they drink. Okay, responsible designated drivers will sip sodas. Some women I know have met absolutely wonderful men in bars and nightclubs. I have not.

Bars present a gamble for quality characteristics, and the odds are in the house's favor. You may not find any one you really want to know, but you'll buy some drinks in the process. Country and Western clubs with dancing lessons can easily yield nice trout in a low-pressure, fun environment.

Singles dances – Some may argue otherwise, but I've only met blowfish, bottom feeders and urchins at singles dances. They can be carefree opportunities for meeting, mixing and mingling, but all too often there's an air of desperation that taints the proceedings. The quality of this stream can vary, depending on the sponsoring organizations.

Conventions and trade shows – Populated with sea trout, reserve these venues for catch & release fishing. Meetings in distant cities allow people to indulge in conduct not manifest at home. If you do meet Prince Charming at a convention, he'll no doubt live halfway across the country and you'll wind up with huge phone bills and scads of frequent flier miles. But what's he doing, and with whom, while you're not around?

Cruising cars – Beware of guys driving showy, racy cars, low-riders, Corvettes, Thunderbirds, some Mustangs, and such. These autos are penis-mobiles that shout, "Look at me!" These vehicles most likely contain blowfish with a testosterone overdose.

Fast food restaurants – With fast food, fast service and fast fish, these places are loaded with grease. The guys are likely to slide out of your life as quickly as they come.

Gail Rubin

Laundromats – You know he doesn't live in a place with its own washer and dryer. Is it economics, a social statement, just passing through or what?

Halls of commerce – Shopping in the grocery store can go either way as a quality or stock and pull stream. After all, everyone's got to eat, and the meat market can be a rewarding meet market. You'll also find plenty of fellows to cast to at the wholesale warehouse, the local hardware mercantile, the men's sections of department stores, and computer shops.

If you've got the money, you can catch yourself a honey while out shopping for something else. But there's always the chance he's not what he seems.

Trolling for Trout in Newspapers

When the legend becomes fact, print the legend.
The Man Who Shot Liberty Valance

A greater number of anglers troll for trouser trout through personal ads in newspapers, magazines and online than ever before. In this type of fishing, you cast a wide net to pull in whatever fish are available. While this approach can be effective, you may be appalled by what you indiscriminately reel in.

Utilizing personal ads, you run the risk of netting all kinds of Other Fish in the Sea, the blowfish, crabs, clams, jellyfish, and urchins. The meeting process may result in comical, sometimes painful, time-consuming exercises. And then you toss them back.

Anglers who hook up with their trophy trout through personal ads do exist, reinforcing this venue's viability. These anglers are like lottery winners. Those who actually hit the jackpot represent a very small percentage of those who play the game, but it fuels hope for other gamblers.

The game works in several different ways. Usually, the person advertising him or her self gets 20 to 30 words for free and pays for any additional verbiage. Some popular magazines don't give any free space at all and require payment per word in advance. Many ad services provide a voice mailbox for phone responses, while some still handle replies by letter (photos a plus). Email communications are another response option.

For voice mail replies, the advertiser records a message that respondents would hear, telling them a bit more about themselves. The advertiser also requests that respondents leave a message about themselves and contact information.

The ad services make their money when people respond to these ads via 900-numbers and pay several dollars per minute for the call. The email response mechanism may be taking the place of phone responses. The Web site administrators make their money by keeping count of the number of eyeballs that see each page with ads.

While researching this book, I placed my own ad in a local paper – purely an experiment to see what would happen. The ad read:

TROUT FISHING IN AMERICA – Experienced angler (38) seeks wily trout for field trips, scintillating conversations, and more. I'm trim, brunette, energetic, and smart, enjoy the great outdoors and city life.

I was actually pleasantly surprised by the results. Most of the guys were reasonably attractive, intelligent, professional, personable, and, as you might imagine, interested in trout fishing. While I cast for trout, I wound up catching fishermen. One must be careful with wording.

My meetings with these men were pleasant enough, and the experience yielded some interesting anecdotes. One respondent, upon hearing I was going out to make music with some friends, said, "You have friends? Uh, I'm kind of a recluse." As they say in the old tuna commercial, "Sorry, Charlie."

I also heard some remarkable fishing stories, including one from a guy who caught one of the biggest fish of his life while in the midst of taking a pee and wound up wetting his waders. This story reinforces being alert to the possibility of getting a strike at any time.

However, I didn't find this trolling method to be terribly productive. The major flaw in personal ads lies in a lack of common ground. There's no reason for your paths to cross, except for the ad.

While we try to be as specific as possible in our descriptions of what we want, these ads all start to sound the same. Don't we all want someone caring, funny and active? I doubt if you'll ever see "Looking for humorless, channel-surfing bore" in the paper.

Cyber-Surfing and Speed Dating

Most of what's purported to be new in fishing at any given time isn't really new at all, at least in concept.

John Merwin, *The New American Trout Fishing*

The Internet can be a rewarding dating pool for the computer-savvy angler. Although there are creeps out there, the good guys are also online, and one of them may be a computer angler's trophy trout. Plus, an online relationship can be conducted without having to shave your legs.

The connections and exchanges made online can provide a strong relationship foundation, because a person's personality and intellect shine through their words. Looks become a secondary factor, at least until a meeting in real life occurs.

A Google.com search for "dating" will yield dozens, even hundreds of Web sites with introduction services, personal ad bulletin boards, and even dating games. You'll also find scientific sites on radioisotope and carbon dating techniques.

There are sites that focus on almost any kind of relationship you could want: straight, gay, Christian, Jewish, HIV-positive, herpes-positive, polygamists, tall people, fat people, prison inmates, and more. America Online, CompuServe, and Yahoo have their own personal ads and relationship sections for members.

Some sites are free, while others require payment for access. Two national sites you might want to check out include Cupid.com and Match.com. These sites can direct you to dating Web sites targeted by cities and regions. Note: With the Internet constantly changing, these sites may become obsolete without notice.

An advantage of angling in cyberspace is that you have the chance to get a feel for someone's personality before an actual meeting, if you decide to go that far. In writing, we have time to pick well-chosen words, yet we may not be able to verbalize well in person. Conversely, if spelling and grammar are awful, you might think your correspondent speaks poorly, but you could be wrong.

The shorthand of email and prevalence of emoticons has created a whole new language to revive the deteriorating art of letter writing. Examples of emoticons include ;-) (a knowing wink), :-{ (disappointment), and :-o (surprise).

Words that connect and reveal our true selves have power, whether the words are delivered on paper or over the phone lines onto glowing computer screens. The written word ignites passion that transcends distance. E-mail notes can escalate into intensive correspondence, leading to phone calls and finally, a face-to-face meeting.

There are numerous tales of awe and woe when online daters actually meet. It can be wonderful, or it can be wretched. This is when online anglers discover whether or not those computer-bound trout have developed their personal hygiene, social skills or other interests outside of online activities. A good friend of mine found her soul mate by connecting online, again reinforcing the notion that you can hit the jackpot through this approach.

In cyber-trolling, as in answering personal ads, you run the risk of reality not living up to the hype. What someone actually looks like versus what they *say* or think they look like can be remarkably different things. Even more alarming, a person who claims to be a man online can turn out to be a woman, and vice versa.

Chasing the cyber-trout is just the latest iteration of an ages-old sport.

A new controlled-trolling technique is speed dating. Speed dating puts a self-esteem protector plate over the quantity-over-quality-under-time-pressure approach of a singles dance.

Speed dating parties may take place at a restaurant, pub or café, hosted by professional matchmaking organizations or Web sites such as Cupid.com or 8minutedating.com. Guests register online in advance and check in the night of the event and receive numbered nametags, a scorecard, and seat assignments. The absence of names protects participants' identities and fragile egos from the pain of rejection or unwanted follow-up advances.

Party hosts get the "dating" started by blowing a whistle, and couples sit down and talk for three to eight minutes. When time's up, the men move to the woman at the next table to talk. The idea is that chemistry will occur within the first few minutes of meeting.

Participants keep track of their impressions on their scorecards, noting if they'd like to hear from someone again. If both man and woman mark yes, the service will provide contact information to those participants.

The jury is still out as to the efficacy of this approach. If you don't hit it off in the first few minutes, you won't have the chance to find out if a little more time would foster a better connection. Miss an immediate connection and you miss out altogether. But, fishing is a lot like that too.

Chapter Five

Stalking The Wily Trout

Amy looked over the seafood in the glass case, pondering what to get for dinner. Crabs? Too messy, with all that yellow goo inside. Clams? Too hard to open up, and hardly worth the work. What about the fish?

She turned to the bearded thirty-something man standing next to her and recognized Frank from their meeting at the YMCA pool. She hadn't called him since they'd exchanged phone numbers, but maybe it was time to make a move.

"Which looks better to you, the salmon, the rainbow trout or the whitefish?" she inquired.

Frank, pleased to have his opinion sought by the woman with the perky nipples, scrutinized the offerings on ice. "The salmon looks good, but I know the trout comes from a hatchery here in the state, so that'll be really fresh."

"One trout filet, please," said Amy. "When you eat by yourself, you don't need more than one," she explained.

"Yeah, eating by yourself is a bummer. If I might suggest, I make a great salsa that goes with trout and have a Seyval Blanc that would complement it," volunteered Frank. "Would you like a little company with your trout?"

"Jeez, I don't know. Are you good company with your clothes on?"

"I usually don't embarrass myself. Don't you live in the Summit Apartments? I think we're neighbors."

"You're right, I'm in building C," she said, scrutinizing him further and not displeased with what she saw. "Okay, two trout filets, please. You want to come over about seven?"

* * *

Approach with Care

If you got hit in the head with a brick every time you reached for a hamburger, after a while you'd become cautious about reaching for hamburgers. So it is with trout.
John Merwin, *The New American Trout Fishing*

As any good fisherman knows, one approaches the wily trout cautiously. Proper presentation is everything. You don't stomp up to a fishing spot and thrash about – you'll scare off the fish. The same goes for trouser trout.

An alert, but low-key approach generally works best. It is crucial to subtly combine being interested and interesting, appearing available, but not too easy. Going overboard in either direction works against you.

With Amy and Frank's example, we have a positive outcome for a scenario that could go either way. Grocery stores are borderline between quality and stock-and-pull streams (see Chapter Four – Where the Lunkers Lurk), so one can never be too sure.

However, since they had met before at the "Y" and they live in the same apartment complex, they have things in common to strengthen a tentative early connection.

Frank was interested and available, always a good start. Although they'd exchanged numbers, he hadn't called yet. Perhaps he was too busy with work (CPAs are notoriously busy people, especially around tax time) or uncertain about approaching her.

For those wondering, Frank shows signs of being a "nice guy" lake trout, noted by his easygoing demeanor and ability to cook.

Amy's approach made all the difference between getting a strike and going home empty-handed. She could have ignored him completely, bought the fish, had dinner alone, and thought about calling him – sometime. A missed opportunity, but not a death knell for a possible relationship.

A bad approach is to grill him on his salsa recipe, personal history and demanding, "What the hell's Seyval Blanc anyway?" before inviting him to dinner. Such an aggressive demeanor scares off the trout.

If her apartment was a mess and she couldn't have a guest over at the drop of a hat, she could have made arrangements for another date, or perhaps suggested they have dinner at his place. That would be a true test of his interest and housekeeping standards, plus she wouldn't have to deal with the dishes.

If Amy's overture had been cranky, along the lines of "Why the hell do they try to sell seafood in this land-locked state?" or helpless, "Ooh, which fish do you think I should pick?" his reply might not have been quite so warm and friendly.

A lightly-presented leader line can lead to a nibble, and a clumsy cast can scare the trout off.

Surrendering Expectations

… we began to understand that the way to catch big trout was to give up in advance on the possibility of catching one.
     Howell Raines, *Fly Fishing Through the Midlife Crisis*

In *Fly Fishing Through the Midlife Crisis*, Pulitzer Prize-winning writer Howell Raines reveals his fishing roots growing up in Alabama and traces his angling evolution toward fly-fishing. Raines relates his baptism in The Redneck Way of Fishing, a philosophy that espouses "the only good trip is one ending in many dead fish." This kind of fishing involves a lust for conquest in quantity and keeping score of how many and how big they were.

Raines' transformation from The Redneck Way of Fishing to the Zen of fly-fishing is instructive for trouser trout anglers. He asserts that by letting go of the need to catch a fish, and fishing with patience, precision, and a sense that you are destined to catch fish, invariably the fishing will improve.

Raines wrote, "But this fish I had hooked by moving slowly, almost indifferently...I had entered a new knowledge or allowed it to enter me, a circumstance that requires an act of relaxation, a surrender, a submission to the knowledge one wishes to possess...As my indifference about catching fish increased, I was catching more fish than I ever had. Sometimes, I felt that fish were flocking to me."

This same thing can happen in the pursuit of trouser trout. When you are aggressively looking for a man, the neediness and hunger you project flashes through the atmosphere and drives off the trout, just like splashing through the shallows in waders.

Just as fishermen always look forward to hooking a big one whenever they hit the streams, trouser trout anglers of all ages hope to find "The One" and land their trophy trout. Overblown hopes often result in disappointment.

When you head for the streams, go with the intent to pursue an excellent adventure. Savor the outing whether the trip results in a successful strike or not. In both fishing and love, approach the undertaking with cheerful anticipation, but don't inflate expectations out of proportion.

Let go of all hope, all expectations. This is the Zen of trouser trout angling. Life is what happens while you're making other plans, and love comes to those who are open to its flow.

Those who don't expect much shall not be disappointed, and will find surprising delights superior to anything they might have anticipated. While casting about in out-of-the-way streams and going with the flow of their lives, anglers may snare the right trout when and where they least expect it.

The key is to live fully in the present, relax, take an attitude of "If they come, great, if they don't, no loss," and *really mean it*. Before you know it, you'll have your hands full.

I don't know how this works, but it does. An angler who's nonchalantly involved with her own interests will attract trout. An angler who pines and whines is doomed to an empty creel.

It's the *really mean it* part that trips up so many women in pursuit of trouser trout. Women are pressured to be so many things to so many other people, it's hard to reserve time to nurture their personal interests and revel in their independence. However, if you don't have a sense of self-identity, you have little to offer anyone else.

While we need to let go of expectations, do not lower your standards. An angler who settles for less than what she wants and THEN meets her trophy trout is a tragic figure, indeed.

Honest Angling

The difference, in the long run, between fishing like the experts and just plain catching trout is this: the modern angler insists on looking good while casting well; while the old anglers, from Bergman back to Walton, were as devious as road agents.

M.R. Montgomery, *The Way of the Trout*

There is a difference in the way women fish for trouser trout today compared to our grandmothers' time. Today's anglers are more open about their desires, although this hasn't necessarily improved their ability to catch a trout. Playing hard to get helped women of preceding generations land their trophy trout, and for a while, deviousness seemed to be making a comeback as an angling style.

Evidence of this trend was the best seller *The Rules: Time-Tested Secrets for Capturing the Heart of Mr. Right*. Authors Ellen Fein and Sherrie Schneider laid down rules of dating behavior designed to make a man wild about you because you're busy and happy without him, hence a challenge to conquer. Among their tips, they suggested calculated lying, such as saying you are busy if a man calls after Wednesday for a date that Saturday night.

Fly-fishing is about fooling a fish into biting a lure and reeling it in for a landing. Trouser trout angling is about making a connection, and hopefully, keeping it. Altering the truth to attract a trout and keep his attention may work initially. However, the longer a relationship endures, dishonesty can loop around and bite you on the butt.

Authors Fein and Schneider guarantee you'll live "happily ever after" if you follow their rules to the letter. Too bad one of them got divorced by the time their third book of rules for marriage came out.

Following someone else's dictates, whether you are angling for a fish or a man, doesn't mean you will meet with success. There is no guarantee of happily ever after for anyone, whether an angler strings a trophy trout along before marrying him or embraces him quickly.

Even if you have the smoothest approach and the most charming lures, unless you've found an available trout with its head up, specifically, one that's looking to begin with, you will not meet with much success.

Trout who aren't in relationships and aren't looking will be oblivious to any lures an angler presents. Leave them to channel-surf in peace. And an already-committed trout happy with his woman is not likely to respond favorably to your lures, thank goodness.

However, a trouser trout who's *not* happy with his current relationship may be inclined to strike, even if you aren't casting any lures to him. Beware! Any trout who goes beyond harmless flirting with an angler when he already has one at home automatically becomes a slippery eel, and you become The Other Woman.

As The Other Woman you open up a big can of worms and put your heart on the line in return for a precarious position. Perhaps Mr. Eel will extricate himself from his current angler someday, but in the meantime, he can't be with you whenever you want.

Is being the Other Woman better than being alone? Consider the suffering of lonely days and nights as you remember passionate stolen moments and pine for more time with him. Think about the pain you'll cause your friends as you bitch and moan about your situation. Your emotional health will suffer as you wrestle with morals and ethics (if you have any). What about the pain you'll cause this fast fish's angler if she finds out about the affair?

No, it's best to seek those trout available and actively looking. Lines of communication get tangled easily enough when both parties are working to find a significant other. Don't make it harder by hooking another angler's catch.

Angling Etiquette

Also, I charge you, that you break no man's hedges in going about your sports, nor open any man's gates without shutting them again.

Dame Juliana Berners,
The Treatise of Fishing with an Angle

Manners go a long way to make life better for everyone. Trout and other anglers deserve your consideration and respect, and you can expect the same from them.

Anglers should help conserve the quality and quantity of the quarry by following a few simple rules of conduct:

• Don't use dynamite. Attention-getting loudness may land you a few trout, but you'll scare most of them away and ruin the fishing for the rest of us.

• Don't horn in on another angler's water. Competing for the same trouser trout is ugly and can result in hurt feelings. Good girlfriends are priceless; trouser trout may come and go, but fellow anglers provide a much-needed emotional safety net during those one-that-got-away crises.

• Don't steal another angler's trout. This can't be over-emphasized. Dame Juliana talks about angling as a good sport and honest game in which one "takes pleasure without any repentance afterward." There is nothing honest about adultery, and both angler and trout are guilty.

• Don't mangle a fellow's heart just because you can. Anglers need to be kind when they let a trout off the line. Gentle treatment and good turns get rewarded in unexpected ways. That lake trout who didn't interest you might refer some business your way or introduce you to a friend who could be your trophy trout.

• Speak kindly of others. If you can't say something positive about a trout or fellow angler, don't say anything. Gossip can and will backfire on you. However, Other Fish in the Sea who treat you poorly are excused from this rule and may be roundly criticized. Other anglers must be warned.

• Don't obsess about trout. In the *Moby Dick* syndrome, the desire to chase down one particular trouser trout becomes paramount. On the water as in our love lives, obsessing over trout can really kill an otherwise pleasant pastime. Your friends will tire of hearing your endless dissection of each approach and cast you make. If sufficiently harassed, the trout will beat a hasty retreat simply to get away from you.

Be cool, be calm, and be kind to yourself, as well as to him. Trouser trout trolling is a tango between angler and fish. If the trout won't dance, you can't make him. Don't waste your time trying to convince him otherwise.

Casting Techniques

If I was near water that contained fish I had not caught, I could not rest. And this often led me to fish frantically, clumsily and, in the end, badly.

Howell Raines, *Fly Fishing Though the Midlife Crisis*

Before you can catch a trout, you've got to make your presentation. An important component of casting a lure is the leader line – what you first say to a likely looking lunker. What kind of cast you use depends on your personal angling style (Chapter One), what kind of stream you're fishing (Chapter Four), the type of trout you're after (Chapter Two) and lures at your disposal (Chapter Three).

A woman can spend hours ruminating over leader lines for that stunning lunker she's seen at the health club or how to approach a fellow classmate. How you cast your line is just as important as what you say. What's a nervous angler to do?

First of all, relax. To make it a little easier to formulate your own approach, these are the most popular casting forms for your repertoire:

• *Forward Cast* – This is a direct approach with strong eye contact, a broad smile, and bright, business-like manner, generally used in non-threatening daytime settings.

Sample leader lines: "You look a little lost. Can I help you?" "Hi, I'm (your name). Who are you?" Note the use of "I" and "you" linked in short sentences.

• *Back Cast* – This sly roundabout approach relies on tantalizing appearance and smoky mystery to present the lure. It's appropriate for parties and nightclubs where the music is too loud to hear what you're saying anyway.

Sample leader line: No words, just a long, lingering look with a slight smile, a raised eyebrow, and a tilt of the head toward the doorway.

• *Overhead Cast* – This playful, humorous approach works with trout who share a similar sense of humor. It may be utilized to move a friendship along to "something more."

Sample leader lines: "So, you wanna get naked in the hot tub?" "Tell me why we haven't made mad passionate love yet."

• *Roll Cast* – A combination of physical, visual, and intellectual approaches rolled into one killer cast, it is best employed by anglers in top physical shape. Roll casts are especially appropriate at a swimming pool, health club, or dance, when you are already flaunting your body.

Sample leader line: "You know, the experts are now saying that it's best to do this (body movement appropriate to setting) like this," followed by jargon about tension, release, torque, gravity, and such. Chances are good that he will pay especially close attention to torso movements.

• *False Cast* – These practice casts are not intended to have any kind of effect. They're used to work up to a perfect presentation, yet they can inadvertently initiate a strike. These work well in almost any setting.

Sample leader lines: "Mind if I sit here?" "Do you know how this works?" "What a beautiful day."

• *Double Line Haul* – Double your leader lines, double your haul! Pair innocuous statements with questions and watch those trout leap to your lure.

Sample leader lines: In a bookstore – "Did you get the last copy of (whatever book he's holding)? I've been looking all over for that. Want to do a trade so we can both read it?" At religious services – "I know I've seen you here before. I've been coming here for months. What made you choose this congregation?"

Remember, excellent casts result from a relaxed attitude. Don't be concerned if they work or not. It's all practice, and practice makes perfect. Mom's advice when you were a child doesn't apply to adults. Talking to strangers is how they eventually become friends.

Wading Wisdom

For all the romantic prose written about them, trout are no less predators than wolves, eagles or barracudas. If they grew as large as sharks, you can bet that wading wouldn't be nearly so popular with anglers as it is today.
Norman Strung, "The Offer Trout Can't Refuse,"
Field & Stream

In *The New American Trout Fishing*, author John Merwin presents safety rules for wading in streams. While originally intended for fishermen, the following guidelines can be instructive for anglers stalking the wily trouser trout:

1. Decide how you're going to get out of trouble before you get into it.

Keep on the lookout for aberrant behavior and be ready to bolt if things get ugly. Always carry "mad money" when dating a new man. Even if he's paying for the date, always bring enough cash for cab fare and change for pay phones in case your trout *du jour* turns out to be a bottom feeder.

2. If you're not a good swimmer, reduce your risks proportionately.

Unsophisticated anglers, naive in the ways of the wily trouser trout and Other Fish in the Sea, should proceed cautiously. Rely on introductions rather than picking up total strangers. If you're meeting a man through a personal ad, rendezvous at a safe public place such as a popular cafe. Don't give out too much information about yourself over the Internet.

3. Use equipment appropriate for the river you're fishing.

Fishing any waters these days can be hazardous to your health and peace of mind. Carry condoms for any expedition.

4. Keep your body sideways in the current.

This wading technique translates to suggest in any new relationship, minimize friction as much as possible. While honesty is the best policy, avoid arguments if you don't see eye-to-eye. Be upbeat, friendly, and well grounded.

If a quarrel develops with a contentious trout, slide out of it as gracefully as possible, then decide in the privacy of your own space whether to see him anymore. I must note, however, one angler I know prefers being with someone who will put up a fight, rather than a compliant companion. Know your own mode of preferred communications.

5. Shuffle your feet in small steps.

Proceed slowly in new relationships. Open up about the details of your life over several dates, not all at once. Take your time covering unfamiliar territory.

6. Don't drink and wade.

Drink responsibly and keep your wits about you, especially on first dates. Excessive drinking causes dating dilemmas and rueful mornings after. Throwing up in front of someone you want to know better is not a very good way to start. And let's not forget the many horror stories about women who over imbibe, pass out or fall asleep, and wake up to find their date in the process of raping them.

7. Don't panic if you do tumble.

Falling in love is like falling in a stream. It can be exhilarating or chilling. Stay relaxed and alert. You may get the ride of your life. If it does turn out badly, take comfort that some of our worst experiences make the best stories once the terror is over and painful lessons are learned.

The Challenge

The trout is a noble and worthy quarry, one which nature has blessed with temperament and instinct that make him a real challenge.

Paul N. Fling & Donald L. Puterbaugh,
Fly-Fisherman's Primer

Trout fishermen often marvel at how an underwater denizen with such a small brain and an I.Q. of maybe six can outwit even the most dedicated disciples of the sport. At times trout are not fooled by even the most realistic artificial flies.

While it's tempting to compare IQs of trout to those of lesser men, don't be lulled into smug complacency imagining you're smarter than they are. They just think differently than women do.

It is a challenge to approach, play, and land a trouser trout, and it is difficult to let one go. When a woman draws a new man into her life, it can be as thrilling as that moment

Gail Rubin

when a fish is hooked and reeled from its watery world. And that thrill can last considerably longer than those fleeting moments while fishing.

However, the art of illusion in dating, when both trout and angler are on their best behavior, eventually wears off. As time goes by, the quality of the match determines its continuation or termination.

It is sad when a relationship unwinds and you realize he isn't your trophy trout after all. If you toss him back or he slips off the line, you'll be a little wiser and hopefully not too cynical when you rise to the challenge and go back to the streams again.

Sure, there are dangers in trouser trout angling. You could get your heart broken or contract a sexually transmitted disease if you're not careful. But if you play it safe, it's fun, it's educational, and it sure beats staying home watching TV by yourself. Now let's wade into the specifics of how trouser trout anglers handle a strike, set the hook and land that catch!

Chapter Six

A River Runs Through It:
Trouser Trout Tips

Amy and Frank walked hand-in-hand past the floor-to-ceiling fish tanks at the aquarium. Sharks, skates, and eels swam by, oblivious to the frenetic energy jumping between the couple's entwined fingers.

On their first dinner date together, they chatted into the wee hours of the morning. Since then, they'd seen a classic *Star Trek* film, rooted for the local basketball team at a home game, and browsed around the flea market. Now aquarium fish impassively observed Amy and Frank as they delighted in each other's presence.

When they got back to Amy's apartment, she said, "I've got something I want to give you." Frank followed her into the bedroom, a seductive lair decorated with Oriental art, perfumed with orange and cinnamon potpourri. She retrieved a rectangular box from a dresser drawer and pulled out a soft blue cashmere scarf.

As she drew the scarf across his neck, its silken touch made the hair on Frank's arms stand at attention… and that wasn't the only thing that perked up.

With the cashmere lasso, she pulled him close and brushed her lips over the beard stubble on his bare throat. "Come here, you," she said. "Resistance is futile."

* * *

Initiating a Strike

Missing a fish while floating is only a mild and temporary disappointment – you have no chance to redeem yourself and no particular reason to blame yourself – and for the same reason, catching one while drifting by is less satisfying than hooking it while wading: you have not really made the acquaintance of the trout.

M.R. Montgomery, *The Way of the Trout*

How does an angler get from meeting the man to landing her catch? Amy and Frank had to spend some time together before she reeled him into her bedroom. Angling teaches us that patience and persistence are key to landing a good catch.

When you're just starting out with someone new, it's easy to get your leader lines tangled. You look at some fine lunker and your brain stumbles. Your carefully considered casts go awry. You think you sound like an idiot, and maybe you actually do.

Not to worry, casts that get hung up are generally not fatal. Don't berate yourself. Just collect your thoughts and cast your line again.

Once you've exchanged flirtatious glances with a trout, discussed your interests, likes and dislikes, you may want to get to know him better. Take the initiative and say you'd like to get together again.

Notice, this is an expression of interest in seeing him further, not asking him out on a date. You want to bolster his courage, but still let him take the lure.

If he says yes, you've got a strike. If he says no, he's refused your lure, but there may be good reasons he's turned you down (see reasons the fish stop biting in Chapter Seven: Whatcha Gonna Do When the Hole Runs Dry?).

If he does ask you out, make sure you first know the parameters of the date. If he asks you out for a fun time on Saturday night, inquire what he had in mind. If his idea of fun is ice fishing, and you would rather bask in the sun on a warm beach, your concepts of amusing activities diverge widely. Don't commit until you have a good sense of the date's details.

A strike is the equivalent of a nibble – you've gotten his interest but you don't have him hooked yet. And many trouser trout anglers miss strikes. Some trout are so quick and subtle, opportunities unexpectedly slip by. Fortunately, many trout will soon return for another try. Some will even hook themselves for you, whether you want them to or not.

Don't fight a trout's refusal and try to force yourself on him. You can't do it in fishing, and it doesn't work well in relationships. If he changes his mind, he can darn well find you. Anglers have better things to do than gaze longingly down the stream. You've got other fish to fry.

Trouser trout angling is one sport where the hunter can easily become the hunted. Given the slightest encouragement, some trout will come leaping after you, chasing after you trying to leap into your creel.

With these fish, it takes the equivalent of repeatedly whacking them on the head to get them to back off. Interest, enthusiasm and flowers are appreciated, multiple daily telephone calls and obsessive stalking are not.

Setting the Hook

The act of setting the hook must contain within it an almost simultaneous act of surrender… It is an act of physical discipline and of hope – the hope being that by and by when the fish is tired of going where it wants to go, it and the fisherman will still be connected by a thread that leads them to the same place.

Howell Raines, *Fly Fishing Through the Midlife Crisis*

Setting the hook, playing the line and landing a trout can happen in a flash, but it usually takes time. There are instances where the bells and fireworks go off the moment you meet, and the next thing you know, you're landing your catch – usually in a one-night affair. More often, though, you warm up to each other gradually, over days, weeks and months, even years.

Just as my mother told me there were plenty of fish in the sea, it would have been nice to hear her say, as Diana Ross sang, you can't hurry love. Ha! My mother is not Diana Ross.

Mom's favorite quote regarding the pace of relationships is, "Why should he buy the cow when he can get the milk for free?" Translation: "Why aren't you married yet? I want grandchildren! I'm not getting any younger, you know."

But back to not hurrying love…you can't push yourself and a trout to hook up. If he's not ready to bite, you're not going to land him. You can just hear those fishies as they scoot away from you singing, "Nah, nah, nah-nah-nah! You can't catch me."

If it's meant to be, it will be, and it will happen in its own time. The time in between romantic interludes lets us more fully appreciate when we do have a lunker on the line.

It's time to set the hook when you've had a few dates, discovered you both enjoy sushi, swing dancing, science fiction, whatever; when thoughts of him creep into your mind at unexpected moments; when you have long, scintillating conversations on the phone; and the interest is mutual.

I love those fishing stories about men and women who were "just friends" for the longest time, and one day, zap! The best of friends become the best of lovers. I'm living proof that it can happen.

Dave and I had known each other for more than six years before we went out together. I introduced him to my weekly guitar group, the Wednesday Night Pickin', Grinnin', Drinkin' and Lyin' Society. We saw each other socially with many other friends on a regular basis.

Over the years, I had several significant relationships with other guys, and he had a two-year relationship with a woman he met through the group. I went out of town for a few months just after he broke up with her.

While I was gone, it occurred to me, "Hey, Dave's available." I had a party upon my return, and being the nice guy that he is, he stayed to help clean up. When a slow song came on the jukebox, I grabbed him for a slow dance, kissed him and said maybe we should spend more time together.

After our first dinner date at a Thai restaurant, then rafting the Taos Gorge, more camping and other dates, it turned out we have so much more in common than we ever realized. After nine months of dating, my good friend Dave proposed on the Fourth of July, and we were married December 27, 2000. It's been the Love Boat ever since.

When you set the hook and draw a trout close, a tango of resistance and compliance begins, requiring finesse to maintain a connection. If you pull too hard, trying to yank a fellow into your world by force, your line can snap and you have the classic one-that-got-away situation. Bringing up plans for Christmas Eve on a second date in the summer is a bit premature. This goes for guys, too.

A good angler will give a trouser trout as much running line as he wants. If it is truly a connected relationship, he will come back, often more enthusiastic than before. You have to let him know that you are still interested, that you want to continue seeing him. But you also need to maintain your own interests and activities, too. Pulling him close in extreme neediness often results in irritation, discomfort and arguments.

Unfortunately, many needy anglers don't recognize their own neediness. They consider themselves to be people who like to talk and keep in close contact with those they love and assume that others feel the same. They are surprised, hurt, and confused when people back away, turned off by their need for constant contact.

One of the reasons *The Rules* became a relationship best seller was it provided dating behavior parameters for clueless women to follow. The book's rules limiting phone calls to ten minutes, ending the conversation first, and waiting for him to initiate phone calls sound like enforced passivity.

For an aware angler who's responsive to her environment, such restrictions are unnecessary. But for the needy woman with no sense of boundaries, this is good advice. These rules curb that tendency to talk someone's ear off and overstay one's welcome.

In the tug-of-war between the sexes, the battle cry of "I need my space" often echoes in the jilted lover's mind. Kahlil Gibran had it right when he gave lovers the advice, "Let there be spaces in your togetherness."

Humans and fish inhabit different worlds, as do women and men. Give yourself and your trouser trout the latitude to move about with an attitude of confidence.

Landing Your Catch

It's all I wanted, that one fish, electric on the end of my line, and, God, how I could feel him, his jumpy on-and-off current carrying all the way up my arm. How do you do, I felt like saying, it's been a long time.

Lorian Hemingway, *Walk on Water for Me*

Landing your catch can be the physical act of handling the trout, or, if you plan to be fairly celibate until your wedding, it can be an engagement, a concrete commitment to each other. How long it takes to land a trout from the start of a relationship varies. If the chemistry is compelling, it may happen on the first date.

However, it's preferable to know the fellow better before taking such a significant step (don't tell me getting naked and thrashing around with someone isn't a significant step). Landing a trout, as well as releasing him, must be conducted with your full attention, gentle handling, and respect.

When landing your catch, be gentle and pay attention to what you're doing. Avoid misplacing elbows, or tossing small projectiles that can bounce into the danger zone, reducing an otherwise healthy fellow to a quivering, shivering, pain-wracked mess.

As a teenager, in a fit of pique I threw an onyx chess piece at my then-boyfriend. It was a bishop, I believe. The rock piece bounced off his thigh and right into his crotch. The result was not a pretty sight.

When playing the line between angler and trouser trout, the delineation of who's got whom begins to blur. Once you get physical, if you've got your hands on him, no doubt he's got his hands on you. It is hoped that you're both having fun.

When the tango of trout and angler becomes the horizontal mambo and you've drawn that trout into your hands, you have landed your catch. Congratulations! Please refrain from picture taking (we'll take your word for it). For those who have landed their catch by getting engaged and setting the date, wedding day picture taking *is* encouraged.

Although nitpickers would say you haven't officially landed your catch until you've officially tied the knot, I believe engagement is sufficient to define a landing. Still, there's plenty of room for one-that-got away scenarios in engagements, including leaving the angler high and dry at the altar.

It's ironic that the two most popular knots for joining leader lines are the surgeon's knot and the blood knot – painful images of cutting and bleeding to join two lines together into one.

Gail Rubin

Know Your Legal Limit

Also, you must not be too greedy in catching your said
game, as in taking too much at one time, a thing which can
easily happen if you do in every point as this present treatise
shows you.

Dame Juliana Berners,
The Treatise of Fishing with an Angle

In trouser trout angling, you can catch all you can, and
size and weight restrictions are purely personal judgments.
However, the legal limit on keepers is one at a time, unless
you're a deceptive polygamist. While some religious groups
tacitly approve of discreet polygamy for the trout, this
traditionally doesn't apply to the anglers.

You can still have an active and varied dating life, but
don't try to live with one trout and date another, unless you
want your life to be a situation comedy without a laugh
track or a made-for-TV "reality" show.

If a trophy trout is nowhere to be found, there's nothing
wrong with keeping your lunker line full by having more
than one trout on the line. Just be honest, to a certain extent,
about what you're doing.

Juggling more than one man is difficult if you're trying
to hide your extracurricular activities. You don't need to
volunteer details, just say you've already got a date or made
other plans. Adopt the military's policy – if he doesn't ask,
you don't have to tell. He may rather not know.

It is less complicated and generally more satisfying to
land that one trophy trout and fulfill your legal limit with
him. But when the catch of a lifetime doesn't appear,
modern anglers do what they can with catch and release
trout. One can always resort to the ever-ready company of
the migratory vibratory trout.

Recognizing When to Toss One Back

Fly-fishing is not a competition with other fishermen. The only competitors are you and the trout. And if you return unharmed the prize you have trapped, then you have both won.

Jeremy Lucas, *Fly-Fisher*

Whether you keep a trout on the line or practice catch and release depends on the circumstances. For out-of-town trips, catch and release should be your *modus operandi*, unless you want to be an emotional masochist. You may be able to keep an out-of-towner on the line for return engagements, but you run the risk of losing your heart to an unavailable trout.

And how much can you really know about trout landed in those fleeting moments of romance in a distant city? It may have been delightful getting acquainted for two hours in the dark of night, but further exposure in the light of day might reveal a person you don't really want to know.

With locally available trout, once you've landed a catch, the question rises, is this a keeper, THE trophy trout, or do you continue to fish for others?

When you've landed a keeper, you can usually tell. The conversation rolls like the line of a smooth cast, and the silence feels comfortable. You feel good about each other, you share the similar values and interests, the sex is good and he treats you like a queen.

When your thoughts are clouded by mixed emotions, lust or infatuation, it's not so obvious when to lose a loser. Here are some guidelines on when to toss one back:

• Your blood runs cold when your Caller I.D. indicates it's him on the phone.

• He says he'll call, and the prospect doesn't thrill you.

• He says he'll call, and you're pleased. You wait by the phone, and he doesn't call. This happens more than once.

83

• You dread your next date and loath seeing him at your front door.

• Those previously cute things he did or said now greatly irritate you.

• You start thinking about available women you could introduce him to.

• He doesn't get your jokes.

• You mentally or physically cringe when he touches you or calls you by a pet name.

• You and his mother discuss his shortcomings – and she brings up the topic.

• You discover he's lied to you about more than one significant aspect of his life.

• He doesn't respect your cat (if you have one).

• You don't like his friends.

These are only a few warning signs for an impending break-up. Heed these warnings and make your emergency exit plan promptly.

When it becomes apparent that a man is not right for you, trust yourself to say "enough" and release him. This can be very hard since women are socialized to be nice, and saying no doesn't come easily. Evaluate the evidence of his actions and weigh it against your values and goals. If there seem to be some basic discrepancies, it's time to make a change.

How to best release that less-than-stellar trout? It all depends on how long you've known each other. If you've only been out on one or two dates, you can always tell him, "I'm sure you'll make a great trophy trout for some happy angler, but it's not me."

Like catch and release fishing with a barb-less hook, he can easily be set free with little damage. A gentle push back into the stream, and zip! He'll be gone. I have actually used this line, and it works remarkably well.

If he's obsessed with you, it takes a bit more effort to shake the fish loose. In such cases, be direct – subtlety is lost on these guys. Saying something like "I have no interest in ever seeing or speaking to you again" is to the point, yet civil. Just say no, as often as you have to, until he gets the message. Caller I.D. and answering machines are useful avoidance mechanisms for the truly bothersome.

If you're releasing a man with whom you've had a long-term relationship, more discussion is required and there is usually much greater damage to the trout and yourself. After all, you've been entangled with each other for a while, and even if breaking up is your idea, you both will experience disturbed equilibrium as you adjust to a broken connection. Anguish, over-eating, lack of appetite, depression, strange dreams, and altered sleep patterns may disturb your life, but this too shall pass.

When you break up, truly let go. Don't say "let's be friends" and start calling to check on what he's doing. When a fisherman releases a fish, he doesn't try to maintain a connection with it. He sends it off free and clear. Anglers should do the same with trouser trout.

While it's nice when a friendship emerges from the ashes of a failed intimate relationship, you can't force it. You'll know you've reached friendship with a former lover when you can talk with him about the other trout you're casting after.

Post-Release Blues

Poets talk about "spots of time," but it is really fishermen who experience eternity compressed into a moment. No one can tell what a spot of time is until suddenly the whole world is a fish and the fish is gone. I shall remember that son of a bitch forever.

Norman Maclean, *A River Runs Through It*

Gail Rubin

We all have stories of the one that got away. In love, as in fishing, there are circumstances where you lose the catch of your life. It's painful. It hurts to be oh-so-close and have him get away. A fisherman who loses a big one stomps, curses, perhaps throws his rod on the ground in frustration.

The frustrated fisherman's behavior physically mirrors the emotional turmoil we anglers feel at the loss of a relationship we didn't want to lose. We'd all be better off if we vented our frustrations like the fisherman and didn't keep those emotions locked inside. A good cry and some hearty stomping around can go a long way to release a trouser trout that's gone.

Not every trouser trout is a trophy trout. An angler can land dozens of trouser trout, but very few men will have the elusive combination of qualities that make them keepers. Some men make good friends, but they don't make your heart sing. Others are great dates, tons of fun, but totally unreliable. Still others will turn you on sexually but are impossible to live with.

Just because he isn't right for you doesn't mean he isn't a good catch for someone else. So don't be dismayed when you toss one back or he slips off the line.

The loss of a relationship can be sobering and sad. Dreams of happily-ever-after are dashed on the rough rocks of reality. But think of the experience as the angler on the river releasing a hard-fought fish. He's just glad he caught one. It's given him one hell of a story to tell all his buddies, he's learned some lessons about fishing, and he's revved up to catch another one.

Although it may be difficult to think of love in these terms, all experiences, even bad ones, teach us valuable life lessons. An angler who releases a long-held fish is entitled to curse, wail and weep.

But if you must make a scene, do it among your girlfriends. Stormy relationship-ending spectacles muddy the waters and unnerve both parties as they try to pick up and move on with their lives.

Among fellow anglers, good girlfriends won't think less of you for an emotional outburst. After all, you landed one. Even if he wasn't the catch of a lifetime, and more so if he was, landing a trouser trout is no small accomplishment.

As you heal and grow, savor your new knowledge about yourself, others, and the pursuit of trouser trout. You can be the Piscator, the master angler of Izaak Walton's *The Compleat Angler*, and help guide aspiring anglers as they learn the ways of the wily trout.

The One That Got Away can haunt you and loom larger than life as the years go by. Stories of trout not quite caught are often more colorful than tales of trout who now inhabit your home or your heart. And anecdotes of mishaps with Other Fish in the Sea often get repeated more than those stories of the noble trout.

But do yourself a favor and don't dwell on what is past. "Coulda, woulda, shoulda" thoughts are a waste of mental energy. Focus on the here and now. As Eleanor Roosevelt said, "The past is history, the future is a mystery, but today is a gift." That's why it is called the present.

If you must let your thoughts drift back in time, let them flow to pleasant memories of lunkers landed and singing streams alive with trout of all kinds. Every now and then a special trout will raise his head. Treasure good friends and memories. Don't look back in anger.

A Word About Polluted Water

One of the most visible and widespread threats to fish, particularly freshwater species, is pollution of the water in which they live.

The Dorling Kindersley Encyclopedia of Fishing

In the 1990s, we saw the rise of whirling disease among rainbow and brook trout throughout the West. This disease, carried by parasites, causes deformities and circular swimming behavior, hence the name. Although the parasites don't necessarily kill the host, infected fish are more prone to environmental stress and become easy prey for other diseases and for predators. The malady is devastating native trout populations and there's nothing that can be done to control it.

This grim discourse is a reminder to use condoms! Diseases such as gonorrhea, syphilis, herpes, chlamydia, HIV abound in our modern industrial world, and a girl can't be too careful these days. You don't like them, trouser trout don't like them, but use them. If you don't believe me, listen to my mother. Mom approves of condom usage if you're going to sleep around.

It's terrifying to get a phone call several days after a night of unprotected passion to hear a guy say, "By the way, my wife has a case of gonorrhea, did I get it from you?" Aaahh! You know you didn't have it. Perhaps his wife was out trolling while her trout was gone? Could he have given it to you?

You live in an emotional hell for the next few days as you find a clinic, get tested and wait for the results. You breathe a sigh of relief when the results come back negative, but meanwhile tender memories of the tryst are trashed in anger and fear.

Now imagine he told you he had AIDS. Sex is fun, sex is necessary, but it's not something to die a slow and painful death for. Having a positive attitude about condoms and viewing it as a fun, friendly and sexy activity can make their use palatable. Take charge – you slip it on him. If you view it as a slimy rubber thing that's the guy's responsibility, you are abdicating your power and jeopardizing your personal safety.

And there are such amusing and user-friendly names for these little guys! A small sampling of condom nicknames include rubber, sheath, love glove, pillar pullover, wienerhosen, eel envelope, Mr. Happy's business suit, Mr. Hardon's dress whites, Freudian slip, party hat, banana peel, sausage casing, tapioca Tupperware, missile mask, torpedo tube, Bismark barrier, and the latex anti-proliferation device.

Once you get into a monogamous relationship, you can stop using condoms. Until then, you too can experience the same exquisite embarrassment at your local pharmacy that used to be reserved solely for men.

And there are so many choices: textures, colors, lubricants, extra-thin, large (!) – the mind boggles. Just waltz on in with a smile on your face and buy an assortment. Later, you can figure out which kind you and your trout *du jour* like best.

If you happen to have one of the viral diseases that go dormant like herpes or chlamydia, be up front and honest about it – certainly not on your first date, but before you get naked. While it may not kill you, getting a sexually transmitted disease is a major blow to the ego.

Practice the Golden Rule – if the tables were turned, you'd want to know in advance. Think about how would you feel if he was nuzzling your neck and said, "By the way, I'm a vampire."

Assorted Trouser Trout Tips

Lacking any power of reason, trout *are* dumb, but they're not stupid.

John Merwin, *The New American Trout Fishing*

Gail Rubin

Name That Trout!

Since the trouser trout has a personality of its own, many of their owners give them colorful names, some of which are accurate, others seriously overblown.

Submitted for your consideration: Mr. Happy, Mr. Pud, Mr. Wiggly, Mr. Willie, Mr. Hardon, Spike, Monster, The Tool, Gilligan (the Captain's little buddy who always gets him in trouble), The Little Fireman, The Purple Helmet Warrior, Soldier of Love, Private Willie, General Stiffback, Pink Torpedo, and the Protein Torpedo.

There's also The Bald (or Balled) Avenger, The One Eyed Wonder Worm, The One-Eyed Trouser Snake, Python, Pilgrim, Sir, Bubba, His Honor, Tasmanian Devil, Love Pickle, Pepino, The Roto Rooter, The Enterprise (its mission: to boldly come where no man has gone before) and Jason (from the *Friday the 13th* movies – just when you think he's dead he comes back to life).

The Migratory Vibratory Trout

Those Other Fish in the Sea can make a woman reconsider having a relationship with a man at all. And there are those times when no matter how skilled your casts or how clever your lures, the trout just aren't biting. When the call of the wild strikes and the catch of the day is something you can't stomach, what's an angler to do?

Get yourself a migratory vibratory trout. These battery-powered wonders have saved the day for many women when the fishing hole runs dry. The more trout-specific versions are only available in specialty shops, but you can find generic vibrators in most discount stores.

Don't be fooled by the package art showing women rubbing these appliances on their neck or shoulders! If women were shown applying them where they really wanted to, these items would not be sitting on the shelves of your local Wal-Mart.

Lorena Bobbitt and Bob's Two-Bit Taxidermy Advice

Men tremble with fear at the thought of being separated from their trouser trout, which is why the Lorena and John Wayne Bobbitt incident struck such a nerve. Surely you remember this woman who took a knife to her husband's trouser trout and took his weenie for a ride in the car while he lay bleeding profusely in a drunken stupor at home.

At some point in her wild ride, she tossed that trout out the window, where it lay in the grass until paramedics found it, packed it in ice, brought it to the hospital and reattached it to it's rightful owner. We're assuming he was the rightful owner. There aren't many unattached trouser trout floating around on the loose. Men all over America shuddered when they heard the news, and comedians had a heyday.

Apparently, John W. and Lorena were no Ozzie and Harriet. News accounts revealed a relationship rife with alcohol, arguments and unwanted advances, leading Lorena to cut the problem off at the root, as it were. Through timely intervention by skilled surgeons and with the healing passage of time, John Wayne's trouser trout recovered and he has gone on to star in porn films. Did we really need this addition to our cultural repertoire?

Gunnison, Colorado, identifies itself as the "Land of the Rainbow," and of course, we're talking about trout. In a sporting goods shop there, I picked up a card for Bob's Two-Bit Taxidermy, *Where You Get Your Two Bits Worth*. When he's not fishing, Bob provides custom rod building, equipment repair, and fish mounting.

On the back of his business card is a list of instructions in case you catch one that you want to preserve for posterity. Think about Lorena and John Wayne's traumatized trout as you read Bob's guidelines for fish preservation:

1. Kill fish immediately after catch.
2. Avoid excessive handling of fish.
3. Avoid laying objects on fish, such as stringer, other fish, etc.
4. Take good close-up photo in sunlight.
5. Make sure and keep fish wet.
6. Rub fish down as soon as possible with Borax.
7. Wrap in wet towel, then wrap in aluminum foil and freeze.
8. Get fish to Bob's as soon as possible.

Sobering thoughts for any type of trout to ponder.

Tips for the Trout

Ladies, sometimes you'll come across a trout who doesn't have a clue when it comes to dating and relationships. While fumbling behavior can be endearing, more often it comes across as pathetic. If you're friendly with a trout who needs a little help making a good impression with an angler, pass along these helpful tips.

1. Unless you've got a distinctive bass voice like James Earl Jones, don't assume she knows it's you when you first start calling her. "Hi, how are you?" may be followed by "Fine. Who is this?" Identify yourself right away, even if you know she has Caller I.D.

2. Flowers always score points. While not a requirement, it's a nice gesture to present flowers on your first date. It doesn't matter if it's a single homegrown bloom or an inexpensive bouquet from the grocery store. And if a relationship develops, you get bonus points when you give flowers at unexpected moments.

3. Don't use your tongue in a first-time kiss. Keep your saliva to yourself. Sensitive, relaxed, responsive lip action is best. Let her make an inviting move before tongues get involved. And don't try to stick it down her throat. Sensitive, relaxed, responsive are the watchwords for tongue action, too.

4. Do call when you say you're going to, but don't call more than once a day unless there are last-minute changes in plans that necessitate contact. Guys don't like it when women continually call them, and it generally works the other way as well. And guys who don't call when they say they will give the gender a bad reputation.

5. I know we're in the equal-opportunity '90s, and that most women can afford to pay for their own meal, but guys make a much better first date impression when they pick up the check. And unless your rendezvous is at the *Maison Beaucoup Dineros*, lunch is not that expensive.

When a guy says, "I hope you'll let me get this," he can be gallant and you can both feel good. Going Dutch on a first date, anglers often get a cheesy feeling as both parties gamely reach for their wallets to settle up.

6. We don't call 'em wily trout for nothing. Eager is for beavers. Be cool, be calm, be rational. Just as a frenetic angler drives the trout away, a jittery trout causes anglers to reconsider their casts. Let her know you're interested, just don't let your enthusiasm get out of hand.

Chapter Seven

Whatcha Gonna Do When
the Hole Runs Dry?

Helen moved along with the crowd of people flowing from the sanctuary into the reception hall after services. It was time to mingle with members of the congregation over cookies and coffee. She knew this was a quality stream, and hoped this fishing trip would not be in vain.

She first spied a likely looking candidate hovering by the brownies. As she moved closer, however, she noticed the ring on his left hand. She snagged a strawberry, smiled and nodded at him, then moved toward the coffee urn.

While pouring a cup, Helen noticed a striking fellow over by the wall, no ring on his finger, chatting with a woman she knew. She sauntered over to them and joined the conversation.

Helen looked at the man and warmly extended her hand. "I don't believe I've seen you here before. I'm Helen Fine."

"Larry Miller," he said. "I just moved here from New York."

They were making small talk when two more women came over, clutching handfuls of shortbread cookies and strawberries.

"We thought you might like some sweets since you couldn't make it over to the table," they chorused, closing in around him and looking pointedly at Helen.

Seeing the trout was out-numbered by several eager anglers, Helen soon excused herself. She circled the room a few times, searching for any other new prospects. Larry, caught up talking with the three women, never looked her way.

Helen slipped out the door without further incident. "Damn, skunked again," she thought.

* * *

No Nibbles?

Now you must know that there are twelve kinds of impediments which cause [an angler] to catch no fish, apart from other common causes that may happen by chance.

Dame Juliana Berners,
The Treatise of Fishing with an Angle

Even the most accomplished anglers can spend a day on the river and not catch a single trout. And trouser trout angling is even more time-consuming and frequently less productive than ordinary fishing. Yet, when we come up empty-handed, there are lessons to be learned about why the fish stop biting, and how to possibly get a nibble.

In the April 1907 issue of *Field & Stream*, author M.P. Keefe listed reasons why a fish might not rise to the lure. Dame Juliana covered many of the same reasons in her treatise. Note how they correspond to lack of trouser trout interest:

• Because of over-fishing.

Too many women pursuing too few trouser trout ties up the trout's attention and enables him to be especially selective. This is what happened in Helen's case. An overall population balance in the trout's favor across a geographic area can't be changed, but you can vary the specific streams you fish.

• Because they are not hungry.

A trouser trout that's well-fed and happy doesn't need to look around. Chances are, he's already got someone to come home to, and she's doing the cooking.

• Because there are no natural flies, and trout not expecting them do not rise.

If you're casting your lures at an inappropriate time or place, you may not get a bite any time soon. If he's engrossed in a ball game, it will hold his attention stronger than almost any lure you might present, short of prancing around naked. While meeting new people after church is good, trying to flirt with someone during services is not. Reconsider your timing.

• Because they have a plentiful supply of bottom food.

With girlie magazines and x-rated videos, who needs the real thing? Warning: those who avidly consume pornography may be bottom feeders (see Types of Trout, Chapter Two). If he's happy with bottom food, don't bother trying to change his diet. Avoid him and cast to a different fish.

• Because the angler does not have the correct lure.

Sometimes, you just don't match – period. If your lures don't interest him, don't take it personally. Cast to a different trout, or move to another stream.

• Because the fish sees the angler or their tackle.

You want him so badly, he can see the hooks in your lures. He may detect a hint of desperation as you attempt to make a connection to reel him in. Be more discreet or aloof. If he's really interested, he'll come around.

• Because the light is bad.

This can actually work in your favor, but if you can't see him, he probably can't see you. Trout hunt by sight, and to assure good results, it is important to establish eye contact before casting a leader line.

• Because there is electricity in the air.

Stormy weather from a current or recent relationship can spook the trout. And you don't want to be caught wading in the water if lightning strikes nearby. Let emotional storms pass and wait a good long time before casting.

• Because there are predators present.

Prostitutes and gold diggers drive the decent trout away. Reconsider the streams that you're fishing. What are you doing in places like that, anyway?

As Dame Juliana noted, the trout also stop biting because of other chance causes, which might be bad karma, bad vibes, or just bad luck. It can't hurt to check your horoscope or tarot cards to see if they might indicate an improvement.

What's an Angler to Do?

Where other fishermen would become more determined, more inventive, more dedicated in the face of adversity, I simply assumed that there were *no fish here* or they were *not biting.*

Howell Raines, *Fly Fishing Through the Midlife Crisis*

So, what's an angler to do if the fish aren't biting, or the catch is mostly Other Fish in the Sea? Call in the experts! Noted trouser trout expert Dr. Sandy Bottoms has graciously agreed to answer a few questions on the topic.

Dr. Bottoms has observed trouser trout and Other Fish behavior throughout the Northern Hemisphere for thirty years. From the shores of Club Med to the banks of babbling brooks high in the Rocky Mountains, Dr. Bottoms has conducted extensive research into the difference between trouser trout and Other Fish in the Sea. This woman knows, in sordid detail, what puts the "ick" in ichthyology.

Dear Dr. Bottoms:

Maybe you can help me identify what type of trout I have on the line. He's attractive, well dressed, intelligent, self-employed, has a nice house and car, a sense of humor, and a fine dog which he loves and adores.

So what's wrong with this picture? After our first two weeks together, I'm getting the distinct impression that this relationship is all about what I can do for him, never mind what my needs or desires are. He shows more care and affection for his dog than for me, and acts like I should be glad he jumped into my landing net.

When he said he was looking for a woman to be the mother of his children, I thought he might be a brook trout. What kind of trout do you think he is?

Wading & Wondering

Dear Wading:

Don't be fooled by this fish's appealing veneer. What you have on the line is a blowfish – an egotistical fart who thinks he's God's gift to women. Attractive, intelligent, well-dressed, financially secure men who aren't Dolly Vardens are rarely available unless they've got some fatal personality flaw, and his is an overblown ego. He kept it in check long enough to get you interested, and once you got involved, reverted to his natural state, one of "you will worship and please me now."

You were smart to recognize something fishy so early on. The dog was a good tip-off. Dogs give unconditional love and won't challenge his ego by making demands beyond food, water, and being let out when nature calls. A relationship with a female angler is much more complex and taxing. He wants a mother for himself, one who can also give him sex.

You may want to duck out gracefully and toss this one back soon. As this relationship continues, you may find that you'll need to satisfy yourself with a migratory vibratory trout after you've pleasured His Royal Highness.

Dear Dr. Bottoms:

I've been dating a lake trout for a while and like him a lot. I just recently found out he has herpes. Does this make him a trash fish?

Finicky Fisher

Dear Finicky:

Those who have a heart and a soul do not define their loved ones by diseases. A disfigured trout is still a trout. A beloved grandmother who has diabetes is Grandma first and foremost.

Herpes, AIDS, even non-communicable diseases are serious considerations in the early stages of any relationship (and you'd better be practicing safe sex, young lady). However, the quality of the person and how well you fit together are the most important components to consider.

Dear Dr. Bottoms:

I know lots of very nice men who treat me well, take me out to dinner and a movie, help with the garden, and even fix things around the house. I feel like I'm missing something. The trout I've been with are nice but dull. Where's the romance, the adventure, the *joie de vivre*?

Casting for Romance

Dear Casting:

Romance is one thing, and real life is another. In the search for that special someone, you may be dismissing a man as "too nice" or "not exciting enough" because of two common mind sets that women fall prey to: desire for the unavailable man or the rascal.

The woman who wants an unavailable man won't love a man who is free and interested in her. That's boring. She challenges herself by casting to trout who are out of her reach.

She wants to expend her energy winning him over, thinking, "If only he'd see how wonderful I am, he'll drop that woman he's married to and come be with me." It's the thrill of the chase – obsessing about ways to get his attention, hoping for his call, and savoring those fleeting stolen moments – that gets the adrenaline pumping. What a waste of energy.

The other romantic fantasy that conflicts with real life is the Hollywood-driven desire for rascals. Sure, we want caring, communicative men, but we also want them to be rascals.

Rascals are those charismatic fellows with a twinkle in their eyes – charming, unpredictable, fun, sexy, a little dangerous. Among trouser trout, rascals are usually in the categories of sea trout, rainbows and browns, while an occasional whitefish or golden trout may show rascally tendencies.

Rascals are the heroes of romance novels, the product of fertile female imaginations. Rascals are characters like Robin Hood, James Bond, Han Solo. Handsome, swashbuckling fellows all, but would you really want to live with all that unpredictability crashing in on your life?

Gail Rubin

If so, make sure you can discern rascals from scoundrels. Scoundrels may have the same charms as rascals, but at heart they are Other Fish in the Sea – piranhas who take advantage and take off. A rascal will take you for a wild ride, but he'll drop you off safely back home. A scoundrel will take you for a wild ride and leave you stranded at sea.

Rascals are not the most responsible type of men, but they're so entertaining, some women don't mind cleaning up after them. They can, however, be tiring to keep up with. Many women will opt for a quieter, more stable man to be their trophy trout. This works the other way, too. There are men who crave women who are sexy and exciting, but will still take care of them like Mom did.

With movies and television shows filled with good-looking actors playing rascally characters, no wonder you're hankering for a rascal to liven up your love life. Before you buy into the fantasy and chase after that rainbow, take a good look at the fellow who's helping you with the garden. He may have a wild streak lurking beneath that placid exterior. With a little encouragement, perhaps you can undertake an adventure that will satisfy your romantic yearnings.

Dear Dr. Bottoms:

I had a date with a foreigner recently, and I've heard that men from his country are aggressive, so I don't know if he's a brown trout or something else. After going out to dinner, we went back to his house and were getting along swimmingly, when things turned physical. We were kissing and groping, then he wanted to "do it," but I didn't, not so early in the relationship.

He kept insisting and I relented so I wouldn't have to make an ugly scene and find my own way home, but now I feel horrible! And he called me up for another date, but I don't want to go through this again. What should I do?

Caught Hell in High Water

Dear Caught:

Sometimes when you least expect it, a guy who seems to be a noble trout turns out to be a bottom feeder. If a man insists on sex after you've said that you don't want to, he's crossed the line and that's rape. The best thing you can do in this situation is be very clear that you don't want to have sex, with phrases like "No!" and "What part of no don't you understand?"

Being "nice" and submitting rather than saying no is bad for your mental health, and you give him a double message. He may think you want it, perhaps even that you're enjoying it, when you're really screaming bloody murder inside your brain. When just saying no doesn't work, don't worry about your "nice" image. Get up, grab your clothes, and get out as quickly as you can.

Those Other Fish in the Sea who seem to think forcing themselves on a woman is okay need to be told in no uncertain terms that what they do is wrong. Sadly, many women who fall victim think it was their fault somehow and carry terrible guilt around for years. If the bottom feeder doesn't get the message and dares to call again, tell him you don't date guys who don't respect your boundaries.

Dear Dr. Bottoms:

I live in San Francisco, where most of the good-looking men are Dolly Vardens and the available heterosexuals are mostly whitefish. They seem like normal trout at the beginning, but they quickly turn into carp and get all weird. Over the past year, I've dated trouser trout who:

• asked ME out, then complained when I didn't pick up the check.

• whined about tracking dirt into his home when I visited.

• got drunk and way too friendly, way too fast.

• associated me with the shortcomings of previous girlfriends.

- obviously ogled other women in my presence.
- absorbed my time and energy, yet provided no tangible benefit.
- complained how I was altering his life after one date.

I'm not seeking these deviants out, but they seem to be attracted to me. What's a big city angler to do?

San Francisco Surfer Chick

Dear Surfer Chick:

Stop dating these men immediately. These Other Fish in the Sea will only make you crazy.

The numbers game in big cities allows less-than-stellar trout to indulge in obnoxious behavior without consequences. If he pisses you off, it's no big deal. In his experience, there are plenty of other anglers who would like to land him.

In this regard, an ordinary fisherman has a real advantage over a trouser trout angler. Either you catch a fish or you don't. You don't get into a fight with the fish, except for the battle of reeling it in, which is part of the fun. The fish won't make you cry, unless you lose it before you can land it and the fish truly was a lunker. Plus, the fish won't make snide remarks to you in front of your friends.

Perhaps more women should take up fly-fishing and let the trouser trout fend for themselves. Then perhaps those borderline trout will come to their senses and behave like civil human beings.

Dear Dr. Bottoms:

I started dating a man who I felt incredibly comfortable with, and I truly thought that we were soul mates. After I fall in love with the guy, he tells me he wants to be a woman!

First he was cross-dressing when I wasn't around, and now he's dressing like a woman all the time. He's even started hormone therapy. While I have to admit he's got very nice legs, I am shocked and crushed, because I really do love him.

He says he wants to continue seeing me when he's a woman. I don't want a lesbian relationship, and I had hoped to have a child before reaching menopause. This situation is making me nuts. What should I do?

An Angry Angler

Dear Angry:

You have a Dolly Varden on the line, a cross-dresser who wants to cross the gender line and become an angler. The appeal of the Dolly lies in his ability to understand and empathize with the female sex, and that is a powerful attractor. Most Dolly Vardens are homosexual, so while they make great shopping and travel buddies, there's little concern about sex and child rearing.

If a relationship with a transsexual is not what you want, end it. You want to have a child, but this is not the guy to do it with. It sounds like he won't have the equipment much longer. While he could be a very nurturing parent, he won't make much of a father figure.

If you're truly serious about having a child sometime soon, make sure you are up to the non-stop task of nurturing a totally dependent being. You may want to start with a pet dog. If you think you can handle being a single parent, consider pursuing adoption.

Dear Dr. Bottoms:

I'm about at the end of my line with trouser trout angling. It seems like I strike out in every stream I fish. I've met all the guys at the health club, and none of them are right for me. I've gone through so many men at church I'm thinking of changing congregations. All of my friends and co-workers know I'm looking, but none have introduced me to anyone.

I've taken classes, gone to dances, joined organizations, and after all of this, I still haven't gotten a strike from a suitable trout, let alone actually landed one. I'm ready to either fling myself before the first available man who isn't an Other Fish in the Sea or hang up my rod and reel. What do you think?

Frustrated Angler

Dear Frustrated:

There is such a thing as trying too hard. Hang up the tackle for a while. It is futile for an angler to fling herself at trouser trout. That only drives them away. The thing to do is change your attitude and get busy with other activities that interest you.

There is more to life than fishing for trouser trout. Besides a job and/or school, a well-adjusted angler has family and friends to be with, hobbies and interests to pursue, and causes to support. While there are fishermen who obsess over fishing, they still make a living and may pursue at least a few other interests.

For example, Renee, a clinical psychologist who moved to Denver, had lived there for months and was having no luck meeting eligible trouser trout, in spite of her best efforts. After a period of despondency, she decided to join an outdoors club and signed up for a river trip on the Amazon.

While cruising down the world's mightiest river, she met the trophy trout of her dreams, they fell madly in love, and (such a miracle!) he happened to live in Denver. Renee had to pursue her own interests on another continent before hooking her trophy trout. You may have to go to great lengths, but following the call of your own wild side does pay off.

Going and Flowing

Also you should busy yourself to nourish the game in
everything that you can, and to destroy all such things as are
devourers of it. And all those that do according to this rule
will have the blessing of God and St. Peter.

Dame Juliana Berners,
The Treatise of Fishing with an Angle

So what to do when the hole runs dry, and there are no
trouser trout to be had? Go have a drink with your fellow
anglers and plan a new adventure. Work on a project that
gives you a sense of accomplishment. Move the furniture
around in your home or redecorate. Take a hot bath and read
a good book. Go exercise and work out the stress. Get a life.
Ignore trouser trout altogether. I've done all of these things
at once. Trust me, when you least expect it, your trophy
trout will pop up.

Waiting for the day when that trophy trout swims along
and you can land him may seem impossible when you're in
the throes of unfulfilled lust. I heartily recommend keeping
a migratory vibratory trout handy to tide you over when the
fishing hole runs dry. Just make sure you have plenty of
fresh batteries on hand.

Meanwhile, go with the flow, savor the scenery, and
enjoy your self with all that makes you unique.

Chapter Eight

It Was This Big! Adventures In Trouser Trout Angling

The experience of fishing with remarkable women was not about how many fish were landed or who caught the biggest trout. It was an unusual adventure for them.

Sally I. Stoner, *Women in the Stream*

What trouser trout angler doesn't have at least one big fish story, whether he slipped off the line or was taken home as a keeper to be mounted for posterity? Part of the fun of going fishing is talking about those experiences with other trouser trout anglers.

However, such conversations don't usually focus on the physical aspects of a relationship. Sure, we want to know if he was cute and in good shape, but frankly, most of us don't want details on the size and shape of his trout and whether or not he has buns of steel. I especially don't want to hear about dough-buns.

We *do* discuss whether he's an idiot, a prince or a jerk, what he does on dates, and how he treats people. While we love our friends and hope they have a rewarding sex life, a poignant catch and release story will hold our interest longer than a blow-by-blow account of landing a lunker. Still, some women like to hear all the gory details.

Let's listen in on Margo, Helen and Amy as they swap tall tales of trouser trout angling.

* * *

"So what was the biggest one you ever caught?" inquired Margo as she, Amy and Helen sat sipping Margaritas and snacking on salsa and chips in their favorite local cantina.

"Oh gosh, I would say it was that French fellow Raoul I knew years ago," said Helen. "He was an artist who was kind of homely, bald, smoked like a chimney and had ears like Dumbo, but boy, he was in great shape and, ahem, quite the lunker."

"He had this thick French accent that would just crack me up sometimes. He once looked out the window and said, 'Youh have skeewerahlls in zee yard.' He had to say it three times before I figured out he was talking about squirrels."

"A brown trout to be sure. How did you meet him?" asked Amy.

"I used to practice aikido, a Japanese martial art that includes practice with wooden staffs and swords. We'd carry them around in these distinctive cloth bags. I was leaving work one day, headed for the subway, when I saw this fellow toting one of these bags, energetically talking to a taxi driver. Figuring he was an aikidoist, I went over to see if I could help."

"I went up to him, said I practice aikido, and he says, 'I want to go to Satomei Sensei's dojo in Takoma Park. Do you know where that is?' Well, I did know where it was, although it wasn't the club I practiced at."

"He had just landed in the U.S. from France, and the airport shuttle had dropped him off downtown. I told him, 'Yes, but don't take a taxi, that would be very expensive. Why don't you come with me on the subway?' He said, 'Hokay, bye-bye Mr. Taxi Man' and came along with me. I had to scramble to remember my high school French on the trip to the suburbs."

"You just picked him up off the street like that?" said Amy.

"Well, yeah, but he was a fellow aikidoist! It turns out he actually knew someone from my club who had studied in the main dojo in Japan the same time he was there. Raoul was a bohemian sort who went all over the world studying this martial art and making wildly colored paintings and furniture. I don't know how he afforded it."

"What happened to him?" said Margo.

"Well, he was here for about six months, studying and living at the dojo, and we saw each other on occasion. He had a wacky girlfriend who followed him over here, so when she was here I didn't see him. He said she was a *sorciere*, a sorceress who cast a spell on him and drove him crazy."

"Eventually, he went back to France and gave up aikido. Even though it's a so-called gentle martial art, it can be hard on your body. I know my knees and back felt a lot better after I stopped."

"Probably because you stopped cavorting off the mat with other aikidoists," murmured Amy.

* * *

Notice that Helen landed this trout because he had the same interest that she pursued, and she wasn't afraid to talk to a stranger. We know we shouldn't talk to weird, creepy guys on the street, that's a given.

However, Helen knew this fellow practiced aikido from the bag of wooden weapons he carried, so that gave her a clue he was okay. He was armed, but not dangerous. Also, she knew French from high school, and wasn't afraid to stumble on the language trying to communicate with him. Her lack of fear prompted an adventure in international relations.

* * *

"Well, those French men do have a certain something I find terribly attractive," said Margo.

"It's the accent," said Helen.

Margo continued, "I once worked on a documentary about Jacques Cousteau and was at this huge party held in tents on the banks of the Potomac River at Mount Vernon. The *Calypso* docked at the pier, and the whole crew was there. I set up my camera next to an empty table with place cards on each plate."

"After a while, a group of well-built, tanned French-speaking men showed up and took seats around the table. The one closest to me, a cute, compact man with dark curly hair and green eyes, looked me up and down, and I looked him up and down. Then I said, 'You must be Etienne.' He looked surprised and said, "Why yes, how did you know?' in that wonderful French accent. I said, 'I looked at your place card.'"

"Brilliant move," said Helen.

"Turns out he was a diver on the *Calypso*," continued Margo. "I had a chance to talk with him later during the party, and on a lark, I gave him my card and said the next time he was in Washington to give me a call and I'd take him to lunch."

"You didn't!" the girls cried in unison.

"Well, there was no harm in doing that. I frankly didn't think I'd ever hear from him again. But about a week later, I got a postcard from Martinique, which read, 'I think you don't remember me. I am Etienne, with *Calypso*.'

"Well, of course I remembered him! I was thrilled. He offered to keep in contact with me and said that he hoped to meet me again one day, 'because you are a very beautiful woman.'"

"This launched a correspondence that lasted almost two years. I received his letters from all over the world – New Zealand, Tahiti, the Galapagos Islands, Ecuador, Chile,

Cuba, France. We developed a relationship through letters that eventually became pretty torrid."

"Lust transcends international boundaries, especially for men on a ship with no female company," observed Amy. "Except for Mrs. Cousteau, and I don't think she counts."

"One day I got a ship-to-shore call at the office from Etienne on board the *Calypso* somewhere in the Pacific Ocean. He said he was coming through Washington on his way to Cousteau headquarters in Norfolk, Virginia, and asked if he could he see me while he was here."

"It was like a dream, and my heart was pounding! This exotic man was ready to leap into my landing net, although I knew it would be strictly catch and release."

"So, you went?" said Helen.

"Yes, I met him in at the airport, and it was just like those romantic movies where they spot each other through the crowd. He was shorter than I remembered, but still *so* cute!"

"I took him on a night-time tour of the monuments on the Mall, where we walked among the budding cherry blossom trees. Then in a sudden gesture of exuberance, he gave me a big hug and a kiss, lifted me up, and spun me around. It was the most romantic moment!"

"I'll bet it got more romantic than that," said Amy.

"Well, yes. Then we checked into a hotel, and he unpacked some presents for me – earrings and a pin from New Zealand, and a decorative cloth the natives wear in Tahiti. We took a bath together, then made love half the night. All the passion we'd expressed through our letters finally found physical expression. I fell asleep with my head on his chest and woke up in the exact same position in the morning."

"So, what happened to him?" Helen inquired.

"I took him to the airport in the morning. As I watched him walk across the tarmac to get on that small prop plane, it was like the end of *Casablanca*. I knew I would never see him again, and yet, that was all right. The dream had come true. He left the Cousteau Society shortly after our rendezvous and went to work as a pearl diver in Tahiti. We didn't correspond much after that."

"Too bad you were married at the time," said Amy. "Robbie wasn't too happy when he found out about it."

"Well, I wasn't too happy with him during that period. He was quite the stick in the mud," said Margo. "This gave use both an impetus to work on our marriage, but I soon came to realize I needed out. I've been much happier since we got divorced."

* * *

Margo took advantage of a work-related event to have an international affair of another type. She also used it as an out for a stifling marriage. Her extended letter writing relationship with an exotic adventurer drew her attention away from a dull existence with a man who would not stray from routine.

Her letter-writing relationship could have hung her up emotionally, with promises of passion never fulfilled. However, because she joined him for that one night, it put a period on the end of a very long sentence. Concrete experiences go a long way to dispel dreamy projections of what might be.

Margo's action prompted other reactions in her life, prompting her to seek counseling and make major changes for the better. Her attitude of "I would never see him again, and yet that was all right" allows her to focus on her next trout adventure, without reservations.

* * *

"Small prop airplanes remind me of one wild experience I had with my girlfriend Kim when we were in

114

college," said Amy. "While on vacation in Orlando, we
went out to revel in some Wild Wahini night life and wound
up hooking a golden trout who took us for a ride to Ft.
Lauderdale and back."

"From Orlando? That's an awfully long drive," said
Margo.

"Who said we drove? He flew us in his private plane to
south Florida and back to Orlando in one night. We hooked
up with this guy and his buddy right before we went to
dinner in a nightclub restaurant."

"After dinner, a band that was just awful started
playing, so we discussed other clubs in Orlando we could
visit. Well, Mr. Golden Trout, who was also tall, dark and
handsome, suggested we go to Freeport, in the Bahamas."

"'Sure,' we said sarcastically, 'how are we going to
drive across the Atlantic Ocean?' That's when he said he
had a plane. We, preferring to stay in the U.S., said we
didn't have our toothbrushes with us and suggested Ft.
Lauderdale instead."

Helen asked, "What kind of lures were you using to
make these two total strangers want to fly you to Ft.
Lauderdale?"

Amy said, "Well, being the college student Wild
Wahinis that we were, we were nymphing to the hilt – short
skirts, high heels, and spunky attitudes."

"These guys started making sly references to the Mile
High Club while en route, but nothing happened. We
arrived around midnight and hit the clubs, danced, drank
and had a really good time. We couldn't believe our
amazing situation."

"It wasn't until later in the evening that Mr. Golden
Trout had a few too many bourbons and turned into a
Golden Blowfish. Kim threw her drink on him after he'd
tickled and poked her in the ribs one too many times. I
dragged her off to the ladies room for a little chat, seeing as
I didn't want to take a bus back to Orlando."

"What's the matter with you?" I asked.

"'I got stuck with a rotten son-of-a-bitch, that's what's the matter with me," sputtered Kim. "I don't want to go near that ogre. He's in no condition to fly. I'd rather walk back than trust him with my life.'"

"A waitress in the bathroom overheard our conversation, and when she came out of the stall said, 'Listen girls, if I were you, I'd wire home for some money and take a bus. Get rid of the guy, he sounds like a bum. You just don't let him bother you. You've gotta deal with guys like that. Tell him to shove off.'"

"We were ready to go out and do just that, when his friend, a lake trout, real nice guy, met us at the door and apologized on behalf of his buddy. We got breakfast, and poured coffee into our flagging pilot."

"Afterward, we had a quiet flight back and got home just as the sun was coming up. And that was the last we saw of the Golden Blowfish. It just goes to show, you can have looks and money and still be a jerk of massive proportions."

* * *

Things could have turned very ugly for these feisty young ladies. They could have gotten themselves into major trouble, going off in small airplanes with private pilots who drink bourbon to excess. He could have set a course for the Bahamas or some South American banana republic and they would have had no knowledge or say in the matter.

Great adventures involve great risks, and it's a fine line between fearlessness and foolhardiness. Yet often the stickiest situations make the funniest stories in hindsight. They were lucky.

* * *

"So many of these guys just come and go. It looks like catch and release fishing is the norm for us," said Helen.

"I had a keeper for a while, but he's slipped away," said Margo sadly.

"You mean Paul?" said Amy. "Oh, he's a sweetie, and so good looking, too."

"What happened?" asked Helen.

"Geographic tyranny," said Margo. "We knew each other as friends in college, then went separate ways as adults. We've both been married to other people and divorced. He came out West for a new job and a change of scene. Since he was in the neighborhood, we got reacquainted."

"He's a very handsome fellow, a strong, yet sensitive, quiet type, brown-blonde hair and a great build," said Amy. "He rides a motorcycle and can name all the constellations in the night sky."

Margo continued, "'In the neighborhood' is relative in the West. A ten-hour drive is still pretty far away. We visited each other a couple times and arranged to rendezvous in the mountains for a camping trip."

"I picked an incredibly noisy campground. People had boom boxes blasting everything from *tejano* and *mariachi* music to Enya and Nirvana. Then a tremendous thunderstorm blew up and people dove into their tents, which quieted things down a bit. Meanwhile, we had rolling thunder to camouflage the noise we were making in our tent."

"The next night we camped at a quieter place that had a hot spring pool you could swim in all night long. I have very fond memories of that evening, floating in hot dark water, looking at the stars, and landing one heck of a lunker."

"And that's it?" asked Helen.

"Well, it's hard to have a relationship when you live and work in two separate cities. We keep in touch by email, and he occasionally sends me cards and little gifts. It makes me sad to have a nice trout on the line and not be able to reel him in. It's not quite catch and release, because we're still connected by an electronic thread, and yet I can't land him because of the distance," said Margo.

* * *

Between her adventures with the diver on the *Calypso* and this trout, Margo seems particularly susceptible to catch and release relationships held together through the lure of the written word.

Distant relationships have a dreamy, otherworldly quality that's never dashed by the realities of daily living. You're never around him long enough to discover he has no clue how to use the dishwasher. Margo needs to find a local trout and focus those energies on a man who will be more than a projection screen for her romantic thoughts.

* * *

"Well, I've got one on the line, and this trout's got potential," said Amy.

"What, you haven't told us anything about him!" said Margo.

"You must tell all!" said Helen.

"His name's Frank, and I met him at the pool where I go swimming," said Amy. "It turns out we live in the same apartment complex, in different buildings. It really started over dinner after we ran into each other at the grocery store. We've been seeing each other for a couple of weeks now."

"What's he like?" chimed Margo.

"He's smart and well-read, and a great cook. He's a little taller than me, and slender, with a beard, brown hair, brown eyes. He's very considerate, and even though he works as a CPA, he's got a sense of humor that just makes me laugh all the time."

"As long as you're laughing with him and not at him, that's a good sign," said Helen. "Has he been married before?"

"Yeah, but he got divorced about six years ago, and they didn't have any kids," said Amy. "You know, it's really nice to have him living so nearby. We've seen each other almost every day lately. Sometimes I stay at his place or he stays at mine. He actually has an appreciation for decor."

"Yeah? What style?" asked Helen.

"Kind of Scandinavian modern, very clean and neat. I think my stuff would blend very nicely with his," said Amy.

"As long as you're as tidy as he is," said Margo. "It was Katherine Hepburn's opinion that women should live next door to the men they love, rather than share a home with them. That way, each can have their own space and still see each other whenever they want to."

"You must keep us posted on developments," said Margo. "Helen, did you ever hear back from that computer programmer you met at the singles dance?"

"Yeah, we had lunch," she mumbled with a mouthful of salsa and chips. "But for someone as smart as he claims to be, he didn't impress me as terribly witty."

"Computer programming calls for a different kind of brilliance than writing or art," observed Amy. "We want smart men, but try finding one that engages our hearts as well as our heads…"

"And has money, and helps around the house, and makes us crazy with desire," added Margo. "We don't ask for much, do we?"

The trio called for another round of margaritas and chips before staggering back to their respective homes to feed their cats and check their answering machines for further fishing nibbles.

Chapter Nine

On Golden Pond: Trouser Trout
As Time Goes By

Margo, Helen and Amy, now in their mid-60s, have
reunited for a Wild Wahini weekend in Daytona
Beach. They amble the boardwalk as they eye the graylings
on the shuffleboard courts and the younger trout leaping
through the waves and sunning on the sand.

Margo protects her fair skin from the sun with long
sleeves, a broad brimmed hat, and enough sunscreen to
block a solar flare. Under cover but on the move, Margo is
especially interested in the graylings. Her second husband
passed away two years ago, and she recently began to cast
about for available trout.

Helen, now blonde with bottled assistance, continues to
flirt with abandon while managing to avoid any serious
relationships. Even though the pounds have piled on as the
years have gone by, she cheerfully refuses to obsess about
her weight. "If God wanted me to be thin, there wouldn't be
so much chocolate in the world," she says, eyeing the
goodies in the taffy shop, including the hunk behind the
counter.

Amy's dark hair has now gone gray, and she remains
trim from her regular swimming routine. She and Frank
celebrated their 30th anniversary in December, and they still
hold hands as they take their evening walks. Together they
survived her bout with breast cancer and his heart troubles,
and they still call each other "Sweetie" and "Hon."

"Margo, why look for a man now?" says Helen. "Most
men at this age want a woman for a nurse, a purse, or a
piece, and not necessarily in that order."

"I believe it's more fun to have a partner," Amy murmurs to her.

From a nearby court, a shuffleboard disk veers off course and skittles in front of the women. "Oops, sorry about that, ladies," a mustachioed gent with a slight stoop calls. "You've got some kind of magnetic attraction there."

The women stop and peer over at the two men, sizing up the situation. The guys don't look like criminals, and they certainly seem interested. Margo leads her friends over to the court, saying, "I sense a nibble coming on."

* * *

But could youth last, and love still breed;
Had joys no date, nor age no need;
Then those delights my mind might move
To live with thee, and be thy love.

Izaak Walton, *The Compleat Angler*

Trouser trout angling is not just for the young. As the Baby Boom population ages, greater numbers of older anglers are casting their lines into the dating pool. After the emotional roller coaster of adolescent love and adulthood's failed relationships, "the second time around" is often a vast improvement for both older anglers and trout. It's a time when anglers know more about themselves and what they want in life, and are unwilling to suffer fools gladly.

Selective Feeders

The question isn't whether or not trout are selective, but rather how selective they happen to be at a particular moment.

John Merwin, *The New American Trout Fishing*

As men and women maintain or obtain single status in their later years, they become what is known in fishing circles as selective feeders. In the stream, selective trout will focus their attention on one type of insect, ignoring any other viable foodstuff floating in the stream at the moment.

Among humans, selective feeders are particularly picky about the kind of person they let into their lives. While selective feeding can happen at any age, as we grow older this behavior becomes increasingly prevalent.

With age comes knowledge, particularly self-knowledge. Older anglers have the benefit of experience to better focus on the elements that really matter for their life mate. Selective anglers may actually make lists of qualities they look for in a mate, making it easier to identify the type of trout you really want and to recognize when you've found him.

Nancy, an angler in her early 60s who hit the streams after she got over her husband's death, discovered the importance of being specific with her list of desired qualities.

"I was looking for someone moral, self-supporting, caring and energetic," she said. "However, I initially forgot to include a sense of humor on my list. After I met a man with all those qualities except the ability to smile, I realized how important it is to list *everything* you want in a man."

Many trouser trout who finally know what they want in a woman will woo her with abandon. Conversely, many older anglers will resolutely hold to their hard-won liberty if a relationship with a particular fish doesn't fill the bill.

Selective feeding reduces the number of trouser trout available in a given dating pool. Jan, a very intelligent single woman in her early forties, once observed that, at her age, "all the good ones" (that is, any trout with all the qualities she wants) are already taken.

Limiting concrete factors such as age, race, religion, and financial status will reduce the number of trout available in a geographic location. Combine those factors with subjective elements such as morals, humor, intellect, and interests, and most trout who might meet such exacting standards are already spoken for. However, the good news is Jan finally landed her trophy trout when she was 48.

Divorcees and widowers return to the dating pool all the time, tossing ample eligible quarry the alert angler's way. The tricky part is finding the ones who have weathered the trip well.

Often anglers reel in a likely looking trouser trout, only to find he's been badly used, scarred by previous run-ins with other anglers' hooks. Skittish, cynical, doubtful and bitter, these trout will go to great lengths to avoid a relationship.

It is advisable to gently let such trout go. After a scare with previous anglers, especially ones who perpetrate ugly breakup scenes, they need time off from relationship pressures. Let this fish rest. Temporarily ignore this trout or just be friends with him, until he regains his confidence and resumes feeding.

Even a damaged, recycled trout can heal and be a better catch than before. Elder trout have had interesting adventures and spectacular mishaps in life and love that prompt learning and growth.

Other Fish in the Sea may have similar experiences while aging, but they learn little from life's passages. They repeat the same mistakes and continue to make women's lives miserable.

Nymphs and Spinners

No fish is more vulnerable today than a bulging trout within reach of an angler with a box full of the right nymph imitations.

M.R. Montgomery, *The Way of the Trout*

It's said that nymphs, the juvenile water-dwelling larvae of insects, comprise 90 percent of the trout's diet. In the trouser trout world, nymphs are the standard fare in "men's entertainment" magazines, although these unnaturally beautiful women are uncommon in real life.

In the stream, trout feeding on nymphs and rising just below the surface causes bulging, a fishing term for ripples in the water. When in the company of sexy young nymphs, trouser trout are prone to bulging of a different kind.

Mother Nature designed human sexual response to help ensure survival of the species. Consequently, females in their teens and twenties, the early phase of fertility, are prime targets for lusting lunkers. Nymphs, those dewy, young females that attract attention and set unreasonable standards of beauty for the rest of us, are the most likely candidates for reproductive success.

On the other end of the human fertility spectrum, we have spinners. In fishing, spinners are the spent adult flies that have fulfilled their reproductive destiny. Among human females, spinners are post-menopausal anglers beyond childbearing years. The latter years can be a time of life when a woman finally comes into her own.

In spite of American society's pressure to be life-long nymphs, preserved by plastic surgery and camouflaged by cosmetics, older anglers who accept the changes that aging brings simply adjust their approaches accordingly. In spite of wrinkles and gray hair, women who have "been there and done that" have an appeal that young and nubile nymph anglers cannot match.

Spinner anglers have knowledge and experience on their side, and wily trouser trout will recognize and value those qualities. Although nymph anglers have physical advantages, the sense of self and strength of character that age brings is attractive in its own right. Unlike looks which fade, a blossoming character only gets better with age – until minds and perhaps spirits are lost to the ravages of time.

Moreover, the nymph continues to live on inside every spinner. My mother's friend Charlotte, upon reaching her seventieth birthday, observed, "I look in the mirror and don't recognize the person I see there. I still think of myself as a young girl."

My neighbor Mary, still going strong at 80-something, is a Wild Wahini I'd go chumming with any day. Her vivacious wit and intelligent charm still attracts men of all ages.

And my dear departed grandmother, before she lost her mind to Alzheimer's in her late eighties, would light up whenever a lively tune got toes tapping at family events. She was inevitably the first one out on the dance floor, enticing one of her sons or grandsons to give her a spin.

The vital spark of youth lives on when we have a twinkle in our eyes, a smile on our lips, and rhythm in our bones.

Nymphs, Rods and Reeling in the Years

In midlife, there is plenty of psychic pick-and-shovel work to do that has nothing directly to do with mortality. There is the business of being married or not, of accepting the independence of one's children, of shedding the baggage of old grievances against parents and siblings.

Howell Raines, *Fly Fishing Through the Midlife Crisis*

The midlife transition is a significant time for both angler and trouser trout. From the mid-forties and beyond, we all face issues of mortality, limitations, hopes not realized and dreams deferred. Drastic changes can occur during this time of life, some welcome and others dreaded, as cute children become surly adolescents, parents get ill or die, jobs and careers change, and usually reliable body parts start malfunctioning.

The image most frequently associated with a trouser trout in midlife crisis is a nymph and a hot rod – a former trophy trout gets himself a trophy wife. Not all men do this, of course, but it happens often enough to give them that reputation.

For women, midlife may launch a voyage of evaluation and self-discovery postponed by marriage, child rearing or the pursuit of a career. The rough waters of the midlife passage test even the strongest relationships. In midlife and beyond, we start to truly appreciate the time left to live, how to spend that time, and with whom.

As the kids grow up and the constraints of raising a family drop away, a woman is less likely to put up with a relationship that doesn't bring contentment. Sometimes having the kids move away brings relief, and the couple can focus on each other. Other times it reinforces how much they've grown apart.

It all comes down to the connection between angler and trout. Some women hang on to an unfulfilling relationship out of financial dependency, fear of being alone, or a fear of facing themselves. Those who still have a viable relationship and want to work on saving it consult counselors, psychiatrists, and other experts. Yet, if there is no connection left on the line, some anglers might be happier packing up their gear and heading for a different campground.

Sex and Seniors

If a man lacks physician or doctor, he shall make three things his physician and doctor, and he will never need any more. The first of them is a merry thought. The second is work which is not excessive. The third is a moderate diet.

Dame Juliana Berners,
The Treatise of Fishing with an Angle

Dr. Joyce Brothers says that all that's required for satisfying sex in the later years is good health and an interested partner. I find this comforting information. The sun doesn't set on sex in the sixties and beyond.

My Uncle Syd had several wives during his lifetime, and at age 65 he met a remarkable woman who truly makes him happy. She didn't like the beard he sported, and for her, he shaved it off. "Ah, the things we do for the fairer sex," I commented to him. "The things we do for sex, period," he exclaimed.

Have you seen Zero Mostel as Max Bialystock in Mel Brooks' 1968 movie *The Producers,* the basis for the hit Broadway show? He's an elder impresario who courts little old ladies, giving them a sexual thrill in exchange for their funding his Broadway productions. From the producer's couch to Central Park, Mostel and the little old ladies he fleeced got it on and acted pretty darned frisky.

While that's not too much of a stretch for real life, one dapper grayling said, "It's not that we're not interested, but sometimes the body just doesn't want to cooperate."

As the years roll by, the specter of impotence raises its head. For a man, the only thing worse than having a fingerling is having a dead trout. Okay, a dead fingerling, that would be worse.

Perhaps more frustrating is a part-time dead trout, which cuts out just when the going gets good. This can happen to young men, but generally occurs more often in the middle and later years as various body parts cease to work as well as before.

What to do if you have a dead trout on your hands? You don't want to just flush an otherwise sound relationship. You can work on the situation with a physician or a sex therapist. With a little Viagra, a limping grayling can become a leaping steelhead! Good results can be achieved with acupuncture and Chinese herbs. You can always resort to playing around with a migratory vibratory trout.

Though anglers have to deal with the pains of menstruation, childbirth, and menopause, isn't it a blessing to avoid these types of problems?

Things don't always run smoothly on Golden Pond. The pains and medical problems that infiltrate aging bodies test the spirit of even the most positive personalities. Lingering illness challenges many couples when they arrive at old age together. Yet those who remain steadfast helpmates in the face of adversity provide stellar role models for the rest of us.

And what a special love that is, to care so much for another person for so long, to give one's all and have it returned in kind.

As a hooked trout gives an angler the fight of both their lives, they are tied together in a tango, exchanging their energies and making adjustments to keep the connection. Whether hooked early or late in life, with a trophy trout by one's side, life's long flow becomes one memorable fishing trip.

Chapter Ten

Happy Fishing: May Your Lunker Line Always Be Full

Man's life is but vain, for 'tis subject to pain,
And sorrow, and short as a bubble;
'Tis a hodge-podge of business, and money, and care,
And care, and money and trouble...

But we'll take no care when the weather proves fair;
Nor will we vex now though it rain;
We'll banish all sorrow, and sing till to-morrow,
And angle, and angle again.

Izaak Walton, *The Compleat Angler*

In love, as in fishing, there are good days and bad days. We treasure the moments of serenity and electric connection, and minimize the discomforts and hassles of the angling experience. Why else would we keep coming back to do it over and over again?

We love the anticipation, the excitement and thrills, the afterglow. Love, like a good fishing trip, generates similar feelings and fond memories.

Although love can be an emotional roller coaster ride, so often we're just like kids at an amusement park. As soon as we get off, we get right back in line to ride the roller coaster again. While it can sometimes make us sick to our stomachs, any other ride pales in comparison.

Once you have hooked your trophy trout, your connection will still have rough spots among the smooth sailing. Even loving, committed relationships go through high tides and low tides, cycles of passion and lassitude.

Don't toss a good one back in a fit of pique because he left the cap off the toothpaste. It's less heartache to buy the non-cap style dispenser than to get out there on the dating scene to land yourself a new man.

Long Lasting Marriages

The sport and game of angling is the true means and cause that brings a man into a merry spirit, which makes a flowering age and a long one.

Dame Juliana Berners,
The Treatise of Fishing with an Angle

In spite of a 50% divorce rate, there are still many relationships that weather the challenges of midlife crises and achieve the status of long-term happy marriages. George and Marion Terrell are stellar examples of how to do it right.

George, a grayling of my acquaintance, celebrated 50 years of wedded bliss with his wife Marion before she died. They grew up during the Depression; both served in the military during World War II; they got married in 1945 and raised three daughters in a strong loving family bond.

He said, "My marriage to Marion became the most rewarding, fulfilling, and joyous relationship of my entire existence. I would wish such happiness for every human being on this planet."

George shared with me a few of his tips for a fulfilling relationship that lasts for the long haul.

Common Values: "Because of the socio-economic and political climate and the outbreak of major world conflict in which we grew up, casting a pall of uncertainty over everything, never did we take anything for granted, especially each other."

"It's important that potential partners both recognize that there is meaning and purpose governing our lives and that self-satisfaction and self-aggrandizement are not the most important values."

Realistic Expectations: "Each partner entering into marriage starts out with certain expectations of the other. It is important that these expectations be shared. Surprises can undermine trust. Trouble begins when we fantasize a perfect partner and expect a real one to pliantly conform to the idealized mold into which we try to stuff them."

A Commitment to Partnership: "No one should be expected to carry the whole burden alone. Everything we did became a joint project. There were no assigned roles. This sense of partnership carried on through our entire marriage."

"In the latter years of our marriage, we did everything together and enjoyed it tremendously. Even prosaic things like dusting, vacuuming, and laundry are more fun when you're doing it together. The only thing I failed to do was learn to cook, a defect that I have later come to regret."

Communicate: "Learn to listen with both your eyes and your ears. Be patient and take whatever time is necessary to achieve mutual understanding. Count to ten before responding emotionally."

"It is totally unacceptable for a man to raise his hand or his voice to a lady. Violent response in any controversy is one hundred percent counterproductive and precludes any kind of constructive dialogue."

Recognize and Accept Growth and Change in Your Partner: "Life is a dynamic process, things are ever changing, and the key to coping with change is adaptability. The kind of mutual interdependence needed for a successful joint venture creates bonds that only get stronger with time."

"In our own situation, after a number of years of marriage, we discovered that we were no longer the same two people who tied the knot back in 1945, and we began a process of re-discovering each other. In doing so, we found that it was almost like falling in love all over again."

Mutual Support and Encouragement: "The experience of raising children together adds new strength to a marriage relationship. It is the ultimate joint venture. My loving bride and I were each separate individuals as well as part of this family unit and we had our own interests and concerns in addition to our roles as parents. I went out of my way to support and encourage her to achieve the things she wanted to do, while she did the same for me."

So there you have it. When you land your trophy trout, which you may do if, as Dame Juliana said, "you follow as this treatise shows you," don't abandon your fellow anglers. Keep up with your girl friends and do things with them separate from being a couple.

So many anglers go off to tango with their trout, forgetting about their girl friends until heartbreak hits and they need a sympathetic ear or shoulder to cry on. Female friendships are eternally valuable and deserve your attention, whether you are single or mated.

The dance of angler and trout is a meeting of worlds balanced on the finest of lines. No matter the size of the catch, it's a thrill just to connect. One always hopes the connection will be the beginning of a loving, rewarding lifelong flow, but there are no guarantees. Sometimes, it's a mistake to make that second date, but you won't know unless you go.

Please remember the joys and tribulations of trouser trout trolling are all part of the ebb and flow of life. Don't stop casting because of bad experiences with Other Fish in the Sea. Have new adventures and savor your experiences. Follow your heart and associate with people you respect and love. Take time to appreciate the beauty and humor in the everyday world around you.

And remember – it's not the size of the rod, but the roll of the cast that makes for happy anglers. May you always have a lunker on your line. Happy fishing.

Glossary

In the wide wet world of trouser trout angling, you've got to know the lingo.

In this book, fly-fishing and trouser trout angling share similar terminology. Here's a list of commonly used terms, presented in both the ordinary fishing sense and how the word applies to trouser trout angling. Mark these pages and refer to this list if you find a word that stumps you.

Angler
Fishing Term – A person who fishes, usually a man, although an estimated 10 to 15% of avid fly-fishers are women.
Trouser Trout Term – A woman who fishes for trouser trout.

Attractor
Fishing Term – Big, flashy, colorful lures that don't necessarily resemble a real insect, yet can still provoke trout to strike.
Trouser Trout Term – The lure of using the right colors and accessories to enhance an angler's visual appeal.

Bait
Fishing Term – Worms, small fish, bread, cheese or authentic insects utilized for lures, as opposed to artificial flies.
Trouser Trout Term – Live lures, such as pet animals, utilized to attract a trouser trout's attention.

Bulging
Fishing Term – The motion of the water when a trout rises to take an underwater nymph, also referred to as humping.

Trouser Trout Term – The way you can tell you've got a trout with its head up (if you get to humping, you've gone well beyond just getting a rise).

Cast
Fishing Term – Various skillful methods to present a lure to a trout.
Trouser Trout Term – Same thing.

Catch and release
Fishing Term – Gently returning an unharmed fish to the water after reeling it in.
Trouser Trout Term – Freeing a man from a relationship of brief duration.

Chumming
Fishing Term – Tossing bait into the water to get a fish to rise.
Trouser Trout Term – Hanging out with girlfriends while trolling for trouser trout (a group of females will attract more attention but possibly intimidate the trout).

Creel
Fishing Term – A wicker basket or canvas bag in which to carry one's catch home.
Trouser Trout Term – A mode to transport trouser trout, usually an automobile.

Drag
Fishing Term – A V-shaped ripple caused by a dry fly that moves unnaturally across the surface of the water rather than drifting with the current.
Trouser Trout Term – When a trouser trout dresses up like a woman (see Chapter Two: Types of Trout – Dolly Varden).

Flies (dry and wet)
Fishing Term – A dry fly is an artificial lure designed to float on the surface of the water and imitate an adult insect. A wet fly is a lure designed to imitate a nymph and floats beneath the water's surface.
Trouser Trout Term – The fly is the gateway to the trouser trout's home habitat. A dry fly indicates the trout is occupied by matters of a non-sexual nature. A wet fly indicates the trout has spotted a nymph or other attractor that has prompted it to respond.

Fingerlings
Fishing Term – Juvenile, or very small trout.
Trouser Trout Term – Same thing.

Hook
Fishing Term – The curved, pointed metal spur that snags a fish when it tries to eat a fly.
Trouser Trout Term – The irresistible elements that draw a trouser trout into your hands.

Landing
Fishing Term – Bringing a trout into a net or the hand after playing.
Trouser Trout Term – Bringing a trout into the hand, or getting engaged.

Leader lines
Fishing Term – The fine, transparent thread that provides a nearly invisible transition from the heavier fly line to the artificial fly.
Trouser Trout Term – What you first say to a likely looking trouser trout.

Lunker
Fishing Term – A really big or very fine trout.

Gail Rubin

Trouser Trout Term – Same thing.

Lures
Fishing Term – A wide range of items designed to get a trout's attention and hopefully strike the hook.
Trouser Trout Term – Same thing.

Nymphs
Fishing Term – The water-dwelling larvae of insects and a favorite food for trout.
Trouser Trout Term – Those slinky babes in their teens and 20s who get all the attention and set unreasonable standards of beauty for the rest of the world.

Outfitters
Fishing Term – People who arrange fishing trips and often provide appropriate gear and guides.
Trouser Trout Term – The shops anglers frequent for outfits and lures, including department and outlet stores, unique boutiques and shoe shops.

Priest
Fishing Term – A short, weighted club used by tweedy British fishermen to kill their catch with a blow to the back of the fish's head (last rites, as it were).
Trouser Trout Term – The guy good Catholic girls go to and confess their sins after a rousing night of trouser trout trolling.

Spinner
Fishing Term – A mature female fly that has mated. The term refers to its spent and dying form, spinning in the water's current.
Trouser Trout Term – A mature woman who's been around.

Strike
Fishing Term – The movement when a fish tries to eat a fly.
Trouser Trout Term – A trout's expression of interest in the angler.

Trolling
Fishing Term – Fishing from a moving boat.
Trouser Trout Term – Actively seeking to meet men in public places.

Trout
Fishing Term – The members of the salmonoid family, all with a short second dorsal fin, including rainbow, brown and cutthroat variations of trout. Close relatives include salmon, char, grayling and whitefish.
Trouser Trout Term – A man with many good qualities. It is also the appendage inside his trousers that defines him as a male.

Wild Wahini
Fishing Term – A yet-to-be created attractor lure that is remarkably effective at catching trout.
Trouser Trout Term – Wahini is Polynesian for woman. A Wild Wahini is a gal who is up for any kind of adventure and a good buddy for chumming.

Bibliography:

Recommended reading on life, love and trout fishing

Books on Relationships and Style

Bolen, Jean Shinoda, M.D. *Goddesses In Everywoman: A New Psychology of Women.* New York: HarperCollins Publishers, 1985.

Fein, Ellen and Sherrie Schneider. *The Rules: Time-tested Secrets for Capturing the Heart of Mr. Right.* New York: Warner Books, 1996.

Heimel, Cynthia. *Sex Tips for Girls.* New York: Simon & Schuster, Inc. 1986.

Jackson, Carole. *Color Me Beautiful.* New York: Ballantine Books, 1981.

Books and Articles on Fishing

Berners, Dame Juliana. "The Treatise of Fishing with an Angle." In *Uncommon Waters: Women Write About Fishing.* Seattle, WA: Seal Press, 1991.

Brant, Howard. *How to Catch Trout.* Paterson, NJ: Athletic Activities Publishing Co., 1972.

Brooks, Joe. *Trout Fishing.* New York: Harper & Row, 1972.

Brown, Jeremy and John Power. *The Canadian Fisherman's Handbook*. Winnipeg, Canada: Greywood Publishing, 1970.

The Dorling Kindersley Encyclopedia of Fishing. London: Dorling Kindersley Ltd., 1994.

Fling, Paul N. and Donald L. Puterbaugh. *Fly-Fisherman's Primer*. New York: Sterling Publishing Co., 1985.

Hemingway, Lorian. "Walk on Water for Me." In *A Different Angle: Fly-fishing Stories by Women*. Seattle, WA: Seal Press, 1995.

Jardine, Charles. *The Classic Guide to Fly-Fishing for Trout: The Fly-Fisher's Book of Quarry, Tackle, & Techniques*. London: Dorling Kindersley, 1991.

Koller, Larry. *The Treasury of Angling*. New York: Golden Press, 1963.

Maclean, Norman. *A River Runs Through It*. Chicago: University of Chicago Press, 1976.

Merwin, John. *The New American Trout Fishing*. New York: MacMillan Publishing Company, 1994.

Montgomery, M. R. *The Way of the Trout: An Essay on Anglers, Wild Fish and Running Water: Principles of Fly-Fishing Drawn from Personal Experience, Historical Sources, and the Advice of Companions, Guides and Strangers to which are added Anecdotes of Angling in North America and Great Britain including the Author's Return to the Bitterroot and Blackfoot Rivers of Montana, and Expeditions to New Rivers Created by the Construction*

of Water Reservoirs and to Old Streams Newly Discovered.
New York: Alfred A. Knopf, 1991.

Morris, Holly, ed. *A Different Angle: Fly-fishing Stories by Women.* Seattle, WA: Seal Press, 1995.

Morris, Holly, ed. *Uncommon Waters: Women Write About Fishing.* Seattle, WA: Seal Press, 1991.

Raines, Howell. *Fly Fishing Through The Midlife Crisis.* New York: William Morrow and Company, 1993.

Sally I. Stoner. "Women in the Stream." In *A Different Angle: Fly-fishing Stories by Women.* Seattle, WA: Seal Press, 1995.

Walton, Izaak. *The Compleat Angler.* Edition with introduction by Margaret Bottrall and essay on the author by Andrew Lang. New York: Dutton, 1962.

Wright, Leonard M., Jr., ed. *The Field & Stream Treasury of Trout Fishing.* New York: Nick Lyons Books, 1986.

About the Author

Gail Rubin, a public relations professional, is a trouser trout angling expert. During her 30-year angling career, she dated many swell trouser trout as well as her share of blowfish, crabs and urchins. Ms. Rubin knows, from personal experience, what puts the "ick" in ichthyology. First married in 1983, she resumed trolling following a 1988 divorce. After years of casting for a keeper, she landed her trophy trout and married again in December 2000.

Printed in the United States
16450LVS00002B/94-510

9 781414 012797